New Studies in the Philosophy of Religion

General Editor: W. D. Hudson, Reader in Moral Philosophy,
University of Exeter

This series of monographs includes studies of all the main
problems in the philosophy of religion. It will be of particular
interest to those who study this subject in universities or colleges.
The philosophical problems connected with religious belief are
not, however, a subject of concern only to specialists; they arise
in one form or another for all intelligent men when confronted
by the appeals or the claims of religion.

The general approach of this series is from the standpoint of
contemporary analytical philosophy, and the monographs are
written by a distinguished team of philosophers, all of whom
now teach, or have recently taught, in British or American
universities. Each author has been commissioned to analyse
some aspect of religious belief; to set forth clearly and concisely
the philosophical problems which arise from it; to take into
account the solutions which classical or contemporary philosophers have offered; and to present his own critical assessment
of how religious belief now stands in the light of these problems
and their proposed solutions.

In the main it is theism with which these monographs deal,
because that is the type of religious belief with which readers
are most likely to be familiar, but other forms of religion are not
ignored. Some of the authors are religious believers and some
are not, but it is not their primary aim to write polemically,
much less dogmatically, for or against religion. Rather, they
set themselves to clarify the nature of religious belief in the light
of modern philosophy by bringing into focus the questions about
it which a reasonable man as such has to ask. How is talk of
God like, and how unlike, other universes of discourse in which
men engage, such as science, art or morality? Is this talk of
God self-consistent? Does it accord with other rational beliefs
which we hold about man or the world which he inhabits? It
is questions such as these which this series will help the reader
to answer for himself.

New Studies in the Philosophy of Religion

IN THE SAME SERIES

Published

D. Z. Phillips   *Death and Immortality*
Richard Swinburne   *The Concept of Miracle*
Vernon Pratt   *Religion and Secularisation*
W. W. Bartley III   *Morality and Religion*
Jonathan Barnes   *The Ontological Argument*
Thomas McPherson   *The Argument from Design*
T. R. Miles   *Religious Experience*
Ninian Smart   *The Concept of Worship*

In preparation

D. J. O'Connor   *The Cosmological Argument*
Humphrey Palmer   *The Concept of Analogy*
I. T. Ramsey   *The Problem of Evil*
Kai Nielsen   *Scepticism*
David Jenkins   *The Authenticity of Faith: Existentialist Theology and the Problem of the Knowledge of God*
W. D. Hudson   *Wittgenstein's Influence on the Philosophy of Religion*
Michael Durrant   *The Logic of 'God'*

The Argument from Design

THOMAS McPHERSON
Professor of Philosophy, University College, Cardiff

Macmillan
St. Martin's Press

First published 1972 by
THE MACMILLAN PRESS LTD
London and Basingstoke
Associated companies in New York Toronto
Dublin Melbourne Johannesburg and Madras

Library of Congress catalog card no. 72–77774

SBN 333 10279 7

Printed in Great Britain by
R & R CLARK LTD
Edinburgh

Contents

General Editor's Preface   vii

Preface   ix

1 What is the Argument from Design?   1

2 Design as Mind-imposed   15

3 Purpose in the Universe   23

4 Analogy   43

5 An Empirical Argument   63

6 Conclusion   71

Bibliography   77

General Editor's Preface

The Argument from Design is to the effect that the design evident in the world around us justifies belief in the existence of God as designer of the universe. Interest in this argument among philosophers, whilst at least as old as Anaxagoras, the Greek philosopher who flourished in the fifth century B.C., is nevertheless as modern as this monograph which is about to go to press.

The author differentiates between design in the sense of order and design in the sense of purpose. The universe must evince the former if it is to be thought or spoken about in rational terms at all; but it must evince the latter also if it is to be conceived as the work of a divine creator. What is involved in this notion of purpose? And, more fundamentally, does it make sense to speak of the purposive activity of a creator who transcends the physical universe? Such questions are not evaded in this study.

Hume is identified as the principal critic of the Argument from Design and his attack upon it is carefully considered. By analogy from such facts as that watches have watchmakers, is it logically possible to argue that the universe must have had a creator? Whilst recognising the force of Hume's 'no' to this question, the author rejects his contention that if argument by analogy is allowed, the design in the universe is more plausibly compared to that produced by generation than that produced by intelligence.

Many of its proponents, past and present, have considered that the Argument from Design established the existence of God in much the same way as well-corroborated scientific hypotheses are established. The extent to which the argument is scientific, and to which it could be empirical even if it is not scientific, are considered in this study.

The author writes in a lucid style and this book will be of interest not only to students of philosophy but to all readers who find the question 'Does God exist?' one which it is impossible to ignore. This monograph does not answer that question but at the very least clarifies what is involved in one argument which has been invoked to support an affirmative answer.

W. D. HUDSON

University of Exeter

Preface

This is a small book on a large subject. I hope that any who may wish to pursue further matters that it has not been possible to discuss in much detail here will find help in the Bibliography.

I wish to express my thanks to two of my colleagues at Cardiff, Mr J. A. Brunton, who read most of the book in draft, and Mr Robin Attfield, who read the draft of Chapter 4. They both made a number of extremely valuable comments from which I have profited.

THOMAS McPHERSON

Cardiff
March 1971

1 What is the Argument from Design?

The Argument from Design, in one shape or another, goes back to Plato. (On the history of the Argument, see Hurlbutt.) But it is the form of the Argument that David Hume and Immanuel Kant criticised, and William Paley advocated, that has been chiefly of interest to philosophers; that is to say, it is an argument with an eighteenth-century flavour, and, in particular, the criticisms of it put forward in the eighteenth century by Hume have seemed to the majority of subsequent philosophers to be unanswerable. What precisely is the Argument from Design? Let us begin our discussion of it by noting some representative versions.

Some Versions of the Argument from Design

We shall take first a pre-Humean version – the last of St Thomas Aquinas's Five Ways in the *Summa Theologica*. It would be denied by some scholars that Aquinas's Fifth Way is properly to be seen as a version of the Argument from Design. Nevertheless, it has been taken in this sense. For our present purposes, questions about the proper interpretation of Aquinas are not relevant.

The fifth way is taken from the governance of the world. We see that things which lack intelligence, such as natural bodies, act for an end, and this is evident from their acting always, or nearly always, in the same way, so as to obtain the best result. Hence it is plain that not fortuitously, but designedly do they achieve their end. Now whatever lacks knowledge cannot move towards an end, unless it be directed by some being endowed with knowledge and intelligence; as the arrow is shot to its mark by the archer. Therefore some intelligent being exists by whom all natural things are

1

directed to their end; and this being we call God. (Aquinas, pp. 26–7)

Hume himself presents the Argument at various points in his *Dialogues concerning Natural Religion*, first published, post-humously, in 1779, though originally written long before. The following passage occurs near the beginning of Part ɪɪ:

Not to lose any time in circumlocutions, said Cleanthes, addressing himself to Demea, much less in replying to the pious declamations of Philo; I shall briefly explain how I conceive this matter.. Look round the world: Contemplate the whole and every part of it: You will find it to be nothing but one great machine, subdivided into an infinite number of lesser machines, which again admit of subdivisions, to a degree beyond what human senses and faculties can trace and explain. All these various machines, and even their most minute parts, are adjusted to each other with an accuracy, which ravishes into admiration all men, who have ever contemplated them. The curious adapting of means to ends, throughout all nature, resembles exactly, though it much exceeds, the productions of human contrivance; of human design, thought, wisdom, and intelligence. Since therefore the effects resemble each other, we are led to infer, by all the rules of analogy, that the causes also resemble; and that the Author of nature is somewhat similar to the mind of man; though possessed of much larger faculties, proportioned to the grandeur of the work, which he has executed. By this argument *a posteriori*, and by this argument alone, we do prove at once the existence of a Deity, and his similarity to human mind and intelligence. (Hume [1] p. 143)

The discussion of the Argument from Design in Immanuel Kant's *Critique of Pure Reason*, the first edition of which appeared in 1781, was much influenced by Hume's *Dialogues*, which Kant read in 1780 in a manuscript translation by J. G. Hamann. Kant calls the Argument the Physico-Theological Argument, and states it in the following way:

The chief points of the physico-theological proof are as follows: (1) In the world we everywhere find clear signs of an order in accordance with a determinate purpose, carried out with great wisdom; and this in a universe which is

2

indescribably varied in content and unlimited in extent. (2) This purposive order is quite alien to the things of the world, and only belongs to them contingently; that is to say, the diverse things could not of themselves have co-operated, by so great a combination of diverse means, to the fulfilment of determinate final purposes, had they not been chosen and designed for these purposes by an ordering rational principle in conformity with underlying ideas. (3) There exists, therefore, a sublime and wise cause (or more than one), which must be the cause of the world not merely as a blindly working all-powerful nature, by *fecundity*, but as intelligence, through *freedom*. (4) The unity of this cause may be inferred from the unity of the reciprocal relations existing between the parts of the world, as members of an artfully arranged structure – inferred with certainty in so far as our observation suffices for its verification, and beyond these limits with probability, in accordance with the principles of analogy. (Kant, p. 521)

Hume and Kant wrote as critics of the Argument. Probably the best known of those who supported it was William Paley, who in his *Natural Theology, or Evidences of the Existence and Attributes of the Deity Collected from the Appearances of Nature* (1802) offered a detailed statement and defence of the kind of reasoning that Hume and Kant had found fault with. Paley's *Natural Theology* opens with the celebrated analogy of the watch. This analogy was not original to Paley; it was, indeed, something of a commonplace: but it has become particularly associated with his name.

In crossing a heath, suppose I pitched my foot against a *stone*, and were asked how the stone came to be there: I might possibly answer, that for any thing I knew to the contrary, it had lain there for ever: nor would it perhaps be very easy to shew the absurdity of this answer. But suppose I had found a *watch* upon the ground, and it should be inquired how the watch happened to be in that place; I should hardly think of the answer which I had before given, that, for any thing I knew, the watch might have always been there. Yet why should not this answer serve for the watch as well as for the stone? why is it not as admissible in the second case, as in the first? For this reason, and for no other, viz. that, when we

3

come to inspect the watch, we perceive (what we could not discover in the stone) that its several parts are framed and put together for a purpose, e.g. that they are so formed and adjusted as to produce motion, and that motion so regulated as to point out the hour of the day; that, if the different parts had been differently shaped from what they are, of a different size from what they are, or placed after any other manner, or in any other order, than that in which they are placed, either no motion at all would have been carried on in the machine, or none that would have answered the use that is now served by it. . . . This mechanism being observed (it requires indeed an examination of the instrument, and perhaps some previous knowledge of the subject, to perceive and understand it; but being once, as we have said, observed and understood), the inference, we think, is inevitable, that the watch must have had a maker; that there must have existed, at some time, and at some place or other, an artificer or artificers, who formed it for the purpose which we find it actually to answer; who comprehended its construction, and designed its use. (Paley, pp. 3–4)

Paley proceeds to consider various difficulties, and then, at the beginning of the third chapter ('Application of the Argument'), he writes:

[E]very indication of contrivance, every manifestation of design, which existed in the watch, exists in the works of nature; with the difference, on the side of nature, of being greater and more, and that in a degree which exceeds all computation. I mean, that the contrivances of nature surpass the contrivances of art, in the complexity, subtilty, and curiosity, of the mechanism; and still more, if possible, do they go beyond them in number and variety; yet, in a multitude of cases, are not less evidently contrivances, not less evidently accommodated to their end, or suited to their office, than are the most perfect productions of human ingenuity. (Paley, pp. 12–13)

And Paley then goes on to develop a detailed comparison between an eye and a telescope.

None of the above-quoted versions of the Argument from Design is entirely self-contained; each is taken from a context and cannot be fully appreciated except in its context. This is particularly so in the case of the quotations from Paley. His presentation of the Argument is lengthy and complex; and there is no section of the *Natural Theology* that is both short enough and relatively self-contained enough to be entirely suitable for my purpose. For my intention in quoting these versions is merely to indicate at the outset in brief and general terms the sort of thing the Argument from Design is.

It might seem an important difference that Aquinas and Paley put forward their arguments because they believed them to be valid, whereas Hume and Kant were constructing arguments partly at least with the intention of finding fault with them. It is true that the critic of a position can sometimes, whether deliberately or otherwise, present it in a form more vulnerable to criticism than that which an advocate of it would choose. I do not think, however, that this is an important consideration in the case of these arguments. Indeed, Kant's argument, if anything, might be said to be stronger than Aquinas's; for it is clearly not open to the charge, made against Aquinas by Dr Anthony Kenny, of assuming that if every particular thing that acts for an end is directed by an intelligence, there must be a single intelligence which directs everything that acts for an end (see Kenny, p. 97). We do not need to consider whether this charge is justified or not. As I have already remarked, the interpretation of Aquinas is not my concern. The point is simply that Kant's argument is so expressed as not to lay itself open to the *possibility* of such a charge. We may, however, just note that Professor P. T. Geach writes, on the interpretation of the Fifth Way: 'Aquinas argues that the process of the world as a whole (*omnia*) is goal-directed like the arrow shot by an archer, and must therefore owe its direction to the Cause of the world. Aquinas is not here appealing to empirical evidence of detailed "adaptations". His starting-point is the existence of a single cosmic order' (Geach, p. 117; see also Wicker, pp. 49 ff.).

Several points emerge from an inspection of these representatives of the Argument from Design. First, it is clear that the Argument makes use of such notions as those of purpose, or of a means/end relation between things, or of action aimed at some goal or end; the notion of 'contrivance' is closely related. Secondly, that the Argument is an argument by analogy is made

5

plain – in Aquinas and Paley by the use of specific analogies, those of the arrow and the watch, and in Hume and Kant by an explicit invoking of the general notion of analogy. Thirdly, the starting-point of the Argument is observation: the Argument is (at least in general) in some sense supposed to be an empirical or *a posteriori* one.

The examination of these points will be our task in Chapters 3, 4, and 5. Before that, one or two other matters need to be considered, chiefly centring around the question of the name by which the Argument is, or should be, known.

The Name of the Argument: (a) Order and Purpose

The Argument is sometimes referred to as 'the Argument from Design or Teleological Argument', as if these were simply two names for the same thing. Yet clearly there is a difference between the notion of design and that of end (τέλος – *telos*). Another notion often used in presentations of the Argument is that of order, and this can be distinguished from both design and end.

'The Argument from Design' is a general name for theistic arguments that differ in various respects among themselves but that are linked by (among other things) the fact that they make use of notions such as order, or design, or end, or purpose. Proponents of the Argument have themselves sometimes not been much interested in the distinctions between these notions, or in the question whether 'the Argument from Design' should be regarded as the name of a single argument or as a name for a nest of arguments. But these are not unimportant questions. We need to know what it is that we are examining when we examine 'the Argument from Design'.

Let us consider the terms 'design', 'purpose', 'order'. As applied to actions, the notion of design seems to be very close to that of purpose. To say of something that it has been done with design, or of design, is like saying that it has been done with some intention or for some purpose. We need, however, to distinguish between design or purpose from the point of view of the agent himself and design or purpose from the point of view of an onlooker. If someone acts with a purpose we should normally suppose that he must know what his purpose is and be

6

acting consciously and deliberately towards the achievement of that purpose or towards that end. On the other hand, an onlooker may see, or think he sees, a meaning in someone's actions that has nothing to do with that person's conscious purposes. And this is true in more than one sense. Thus, the onlooker's point of view may be that of someone seeing the 'real' purpose of an action, which is different from what the agent thinks is his purpose (compare Freudian unconscious motives). But it may be something much less dramatic: the movements of a practised ballroom dancer or a skater – or, indeed, those of anyone expertly performing a familiar task – may be largely 'unconscious', as we say; and when an onlooker sees design, or 'meaning', in these movements it is not necessary to suppose that everything he sees must be explained in terms of conscious purposes of the dancer or skater at that time.

As far as things other than actions (and, we must add, the results or products of actions) are concerned, the notion of purpose generally seems out of place; but that of design certainly does not. Design need not be to an end, or for a purpose. There is a sense of 'design' where it is largely synonymous with 'order' or 'pattern', and order or pattern need not be *for* anything. There is order in the arrangement of the colours in the spectrum, but we are not compelled to find some purpose in it. There is unquestionably order of some kind in the arrangement of the books on my bookshelves; but the order is one that someone may find in them or mentally impose on them and not, as it happens, one that is the result of any conscious purpose on my part, though, of course, it might have been. Design, where it means 'merely' order, does not necessarily imply a designer. Given an instance of design it is not always to the point to put the question, 'What is the aim in view, the purpose?' The designs formed in a kaleidoscope are not, as individual designs, designed by anyone for a specific purpose, though the possibility of them is no doubt to be explained in terms of someone's purpose. Meeting the same old schoolfriend in a strange town three years running at 11 a.m. on the anniversary of the accession of Queen Victoria may be coincidence: there need be no purpose here, but this series of incidents can certainly be said to exhibit a pattern, an order, a design.

'Order' is probably in fact slightly ambiguous, though not to the extent that 'design' is: we can say that things are ordered or

7

that they are orderly; and here the former might seem to some to imply an orderer while the latter does not. On the whole, however, 'order' seems much more neutral in this matter than 'design', and I shall therefore take it that 'order' never carries an implication of an orderer. 'Design', however, sometimes does, sometimes does not, carry an implication of a designer.

Let us, for convenience, indicate the sense of 'design' where it is more or less synonymous with 'order' and neutral in the matter of a designer, by using the term 'design-A'. Let us similarly use the term 'design-B' to indicate the sense or senses of 'design' where 'design' is more or less synonymous with 'purpose' or where it is used with reference to adaptations of means to ends. Design in the sense of design-B is sometimes taken to imply a designer. There are, of course, differences between the notions of purpose and means/end, but for the present the distinction I want to call attention to is the basic one between 'mere' order (design-A) and purpose-and-related-notions (design-B). Some further refinement on the notion of design-B is needed, but consideration of this can be postponed.

The name 'Argument from Design' is ambiguous, because the notion of design is itself ambiguous. Where 'design' is taken in the sense 'design-B' there is no great need to distinguish between 'Argument from Design' and 'Teleological Argument': these names can reasonably be regarded as synonyms. But where the sense of 'design' is 'design-A' there is a real distinction between 'Argument from Design' and 'Teleological Argument'. The point can perhaps be driven home by the following consideration. An objection sometimes made to the Argument from Design is that it assumes what has to be proved. It is claimed that if someone says that he sees design in the universe he is doing much more than merely beginning an argument to God. To choose this way of putting the matter is already to be assuming God, for (it is claimed) design implies a designer. It is not difficult, from such a beginning, to conclude to God; but the argument (it would be said) is a put-up job. Now it is clear that as an objection to the Argument from Design this could only apply to the Teleological Argument, or Argument from Design-B, and not to the Argument from Design-A. An argument constructed on the idea that the universe exhibits order (as opposed to purpose) is not open to the charge of smuggling its conclusion into its premisses.

8

It is clear then that there is a distinction to be drawn between 'Teleological Argument' and 'Argument from Design'; for the latter is capable of being interpreted as 'Argument from Design-A'. The ambiguity of 'design' – its link on the one side with conscious purpose and on the other with 'mere' order – means that it cannot always be a matter of indifference whether we use the name 'Argument from Design' or the name 'Teleological Argument'. A teleological argument to God is a line of thought that tends to see the universe as the field of purposive action: with this we are half-way to God already. An argument from design may be the same. On the other hand, it may be a line of thought that sees the universe as exhibiting order (regularity, pattern) but where some considerable effort of reasoning is still required to get from this recognition to God. In practice, it may well be that Arguments from Design have a tendency to trade on the ambiguity of 'design'.

The Name of the Argument: (b) from and to Design

It has frequently been suggested that the Argument should be called not the Argument *from* Design but the Argument *to* Design. The reasoning behind this, as before, has to do with whether the Argument assumes its own conclusion. In the sense of 'design' where we may be inclined to say that design implies a designer, to acknowledge the presence of design in the universe is virtually to have arrived already at the conclusion that there is a divine designer. So what really needs to be established, it is claimed, is not that if the universe exhibits design it must have a designer, but that it does exhibit design in the first place. What is needed is an argument *from* order *to* design; that is, an argument that will show that the order exhibited in the universe is of the kind called design: if that is established the question of God can largely take care of itself.

In the terminology that I have adopted the issue here can be stated as follows. The Argument from Design, so-called, can be said to be both an argument from, and an argument to, design. It is an argument from design-A to design-B. Now the ambiguity of 'design' is not always noted in popular presentations of the Argument. My impression of popular or semi-popular apologetic writing, in so far as it makes use of the Argument from Design, is that writers discuss at length what they take to be

9

evidence of design in nature – the argument in their hands, indeed, largely consisting in a full and detailed presentation of evidence – but that, in general, they do not make any particular distinction between evidence of design-A and evidence of design-B.

It does not seem to me possible to give a simple final pronouncement on the view that the Argument is 'really' an argument *to* design. It might be suggested that its proponents *ought* to develop it exclusively as an argument to design, so as to avoid the charge of assuming its own conclusion; but although this might make for tidiness it would also impose a limitation on the Argument that its proponents might be unwilling to accept.

The possibilities (assuming argument from particular parts of the universe) would seem to be as follows:

(1) argument from design-A direct to a designer;
(2) argument from design-A to design-B, with a final step to a designer;
(3) argument from design-B to a designer;
(4) argument from design-A and design-B, taken together and not distinguished, to a designer.

Of these possible ways of proceeding, (1) is the 'purest', in that it is not open to the charge that the conclusion is assumed; (2) combines richness with tidiness in that it makes use of both kinds of design without confusing them; (3) is the version of which the critic will say that it assumes what it is supposed to prove; (4) is rich but untidy in that it uses both kinds of design but confuses them.

The natural advice to give a would-be user of the Argument would seem to be that (1) is a difficult line to follow and that (2) is for this reason preferable to it; that (3) offers an easier line than (2) but one that may be suspiciously too easy; and that (4) is inadvisable because it confuses things that ought to be distinguished. In practice, (2) and (3) are the lines that have most commonly been adopted in serious philosophical presentations of the Argument, such as those quoted at the beginning of the chapter.

Some Questions

We have been concerned with the name, or names, of the Argument from Design. But the issues involved here are, of course, more than merely terminological; otherwise we should hardly be justified in spending time on them. In addition to the points already noted, the following questions seem to arise out of the foregoing discussion of the name of the Argument.

(1) Reference has been made to 'evidence' of design. The question might be put whether there are important differences between evidence for design-A and evidence for design-B. It may seem on the face of it a plausible suggestion that design-B cannot be directly observed whereas design-A can; that we can directly observe order or pattern but that to detect purpose requires more than observation. I do not think that there is in fact any important difference here, but it seems at least possible that an assumption that there is such a difference may lie behind the criticism of the Argument which says that it is 'really' an argument to and not from design. The Argument, as we have noted, is in some sense an *empirical* argument to God: as an empirical argument it must find its starting-point in something empirically knowable. Its starting-point, we may say, is design; but 'design', as we have seen, is ambiguous. An objection some-times brought – unfairly – against Paley is that he supposes that you could directly observe purpose (design-B) in artefacts. This would be a foolish supposition for Paley or anyone else to make, for you could not know that a watch, supposing you had never seen a watch before, had been designed to serve a purpose unless you had some prior knowledge of machinery – a point that Paley himself was not unaware of. We should not be able to see that the watch exhibited purpose without, as Paley put it, 'an examination of the instrument, and perhaps some previous knowledge of the subject'. Some knowledge and reflection is normally needed before we recognise design-B. We can say then if we like that design-B needs to be argued to. It is possible that those critics of the Argument from Design who offer as an objection to the Argument the fact (as they take it to be) that it is 'really' an Argument *to* Design, are at least in part determined in this direction by a combined assumption that the Argument must be seen as an empirical argument and that design (mean-ing design-B) in the universe cannot be the *starting-point* of an empirical argument because such design cannot be directly observed, but must itself be argued to; it must come in the conclusion and not in the premisses of the Argument, if the Argument is to be an empirical argument. It is surely the case,

however, that reflection, and even argument, may sometimes be needed before design-A is seen, just as (though probably more often) it may be needed before design-B is seen. Some patterns are more obvious than others.

(2) If it were possible to provide an acceptable account of design-B, or some aspect of it, on which it was clear that it did not necessarily involve a designer, then 'Argument *to* Design' (i.e. to design-B) would not after all, as critics have supposed, be a more adequate name than 'Argument *from* Design': for, having established, if we could, that the universe exhibited design-B, we should still need to *argue* from this to a designer; we should be little better off than if we had offered an argument from design-A. How far design-B does necessarily imply a designer is a question that we shall be taking up in Chapters 3 and 4.

(3) We have already noted a sense in which the Argument might be said to be both from and to design. There is another sense in which this might be said. This can be brought out by a reference to both Paley, as a proponent of the Argument, and Kant, as a critic of it. It is commonly supposed that the Argument from Design is put forward as an argument to convince the non-believer of the existence of God. No doubt it has often been intended in this way. Those who discuss the Argument (for example, authors of philosophical textbooks) commonly suppose that this is the only intention lying behind it; and they further suppose that if the Argument can be shown not to be a valid argument to the existence of God – an argument capable of convincing someone not already predisposed to belief in God – then nothing further needs to be said about it. But this is not by any means the end of the matter. Such a proponent of the Argument as Paley recognised that it had a value for the believer in God that it could not have for the non-believer – a religious value – and that the Argument is not adequately understood if it is seen as no more than an attempt to prove God to the non-believer. A constant review of the evidence of design in the universe helps to confirm the believer in a certain attitude:

Now it is by frequent or continued meditation upon a subject, by placing a subject in different points of view, by induction of particulars, by variety of examples, by applying principles to the solution of phenomena, by dwelling upon proofs and

12

consequences, that mental exercise is drawn into any particular channel. It is by these means, at least, that we have any
power over it. The train of spontaneous thought, and the
choice of that train, may be directed to different ends, and
may appear to be more or less judiciously fixed, according
to the purpose in respect of which we consider it: but, in a
moral view, I shall not, I believe, be contradicted when I say,
that if one train of thinking be more desirable than another,
it is that which regards the phenomena of nature with a
constant reference to a supreme intelligent Author. To have
made this the ruling, the habitual sentiment of our minds,
is to have laid the foundation of every thing which is religious.
The world thenceforth becomes a temple, and life itself one
continued act of adoration. The change is no less than this:
that whereas formerly God was seldom in our thoughts, we
can now scarcely look upon any thing without perceiving its
relation to him. (Paley, pp. 316–17)

And Kant indicates that he sees something like this kind of value
in the Argument from Design when he writes of it:

It enlivens the study of nature, just as it itself derives its
existence and gains ever new vigour from that source. It
suggests ends and purposes, where our observation would not
have detected them by itself, and extends our knowledge of
nature by means of the guiding-concept of a special unity,
the principle of which is outside nature. This knowledge again
reacts on its cause, namely, upon the idea which has led to it,
and so strengthens the belief in a supreme Author [of nature]
that the belief acquires the force of an irresistible conviction.
(Kant, p. 520)

The Argument can be seen as both depending upon and
leading to the discovery of design. To the believer in God as
designer, evidence of design is to be found without difficulty
throughout the universe. How could it not be found – for (the
believer will say) is not the universe God's handiwork? And
reciprocally, this evidence of design helps to confirm the
believer's belief in God as designer. In this sense, then, the
Argument can be said to be both from and to design.

13

2 Design as Mind-imposed

When we look about us we see evidence of design. So the Argument from Design tells us. Is it possible, however, that this design is not really there, but that we somehow read it into our experience? (This view is to be distinguished from the view that the Argument may depend on prior belief in the sense that we are able to see design in the universe (only) if we first believe in God as supreme designer. That view does not assume that design is not really there. Quite the contrary.)

If design is 'not really there' but is 'mind-imposed', then the force of the Argument as a proof of God is surely much weakened. Some might say that it would cease altogether to work as a proof.

This doubt can be expressed in terms of either of the two senses of 'design' that we have distinguished. Let us begin with design-A.

Is Design-A Mind-imposed?

It seems that the kind of order that people find in their experience can vary from culture to culture. Thus, in Welsh the word for grass is *glaswellt* (literally: *blue* hay); the word for fortnight is *pythefnos* (literally: *fifteen* night); the word for minute (*munud*) is masculine in the North and feminine in the South. There are primitive languages in which there are no specific words for numbers above three or four, but simply a word meaning something like 'many' or 'a lot'. Facts such as these are presumably evidence that some peoples see things differently from others: people brought up to speak these languages would order their experience to some extent differently from English speakers. To a Ptolemaic astronomer the universe would have exhibited order of a certain kind, an order that we should say was determined by that astronomer's beliefs, whereas to a Copernican astronomer it exhibits order of a different kind. And there are not just cultural variations; there are variations as between

15

person and person: for instance, some individuals are colour-blind. And, further, any single individual can see things some-times one way, sometimes another: consider optical illusions, like that in which a drawing of a cube is seen as extending sometimes in one direction and sometimes in another, or that in which a drawing can be seen at one time as a duck's head and at another as a rabbit's. Just as we observe the regular rising and setting of the sun, so, it seems, do we observe that men have the power to find one kind of order in experience at one time or place and another at another. This certainly does not help the theist who wants to develop an argument from design, and to the extent that the existence of such differences throws doubt on the idea that there is a right way of ordering things, it on the whole would seem to tend against the view that there is a supreme orderer.

At the same time, variations in men's ways of ordering ex-perience do not constitute a really serious objection to the Argument from Design. These variations certainly suggest that the view of the universe as a collection of brute facts, waiting, unchanging, for us to experience them, is altogether too simple. But the existence of variations in ways of ordering experience cannot be taken to show that there are not in fact patterns in nature. There are no doubt more patterns in things than people have sometimes supposed; but, as far as anything so far noted is concerned, patterns are still there from which to choose. The considerations that we have adduced would not warrant the conclusion that there are no patterns at all – that order is purely *created* by ourselves. All that is implied in the foregoing is simply that as a matter of empirical fact there is an element of imposition by the mind (to adopt a convenient way of expressing it) in our experience of things. This view can be formulated in various ways; but our concern here is merely with a *kind* of view, not with differences between various sub-varieties of it. The essential point, as far as we are concerned, is that any view of this kind does not constitute a serious difficulty for the Argument from Design; though, as we have noted, it certainly does not render that Argument any assistance.

However, there is another view, which needs to be distin-guished from that which we have so far noted, according to which, once again, order might be said to be mind-dependent, but where this is seen not merely as an empirical fact about

16

experience but as something much stronger. On the view we are now to consider, it is not the case that the recognition of one kind of order rather than another is, as a matter of fact and to some extent, a question of how we see things. The stronger view I am referring to is that of Kant. In the view of Kant, in the *Critique of Pure Reason*, although the existence of things (that is, of 'things-in-themselves') is not mind-dependent, the categories in terms of which we order our experience of them – such categories as unity and plurality, cause and effect – are supplied by the understanding. Their basic ordering in time and space is also supplied by us. For Kant, order, or design-A as we are calling it, in nature is mind-dependent in a particular sense. What is presented to us in experience is an undifferentiated manifold. The understanding imposes its categories upon this manifold and thus *creates* ordered experience. The reason why this Kantian view can be said to offer a much more serious challenge to the Argument from Design than the view already noted is that Kant is making the radical suggestion that experience *as such* (not this kind of experience as opposed to that) is 'mind-dependent'. The Kantian challenge can, I think, be answered, and we shall consider shortly what might be said against it; but it is important that it should not be ignored. If Kant were correct he would have confronted the Argument from Design with a difficulty of an absolutely fundamental character. The Argument from Design bases itself upon evidence of order in the universe. But what if there is really *no sense* in the notion of order as a feature of things-in-themselves? What if ordered experience is essentially a creation of the categories of our understanding?

Someone might try to meet Kant's challenge by saying that his doctrine does not destroy the Argument from Design but merely alters the terms in which it must be put. That is, whereas the Argument from Design attempts to argue to God from observations of order in nature, could it not shift its ground, someone might be tempted to say, and argue from observations of the design-imposing functions of the forms of sensibility (space and time) and of the understanding? But this will not do. There cannot be *evidence* for these design-imposing powers. We cannot *observe* the design-imposing functions as we can, through them, observe things. On Kant's principles, there would be no sense in the supposition that evidence of design might be evidence of the human power of ordering things, and that the more evidence of design-A that should be presented the clearer would become the conclusion that human beings are very good at organising experience; so that perhaps we might eventually be able to conclude that the power of organising things of which we have so much evidence indicates a supreme designer or orderer who has provided the power. Such a line of reasoning would simply not be intelligible on Kantian principles. Kant does not suppose that there is *evidence* for the existence or the functioning of the categories. The status of the Kantian categories is *a priori*. That we possess the categories is not something for which it makes sense to suppose that we could have empirical evidence. It is not an item of knowledge, acquired by inductive methods and capable of being more fully confirmed by further experience. The categories, Kant holds, are (like space and time) *conditions* of the experience we have, and it is logically absurd to suppose that the conditions of experience might themselves be known through experience. Yet the Argument from Design, as we know, is based upon *evidence* of design. The Kantian view is not the view that there is *evidence* of human ordering powers. This attempt to meet Kant's challenge must therefore be seen as misinterpreting either Kant or the Argument from Design. (It does, however, contain the seeds of a possible, partial, answer to Kant, as we shall shortly see.)

Unlike Kant's view, the milder view that we considered first – that the kind of order people perceive seems to vary in accordance with cultural and other differences – does not imply that there is any logical absurdity in supposing that we might argue to God from observations of human design-imposing powers. It would be an unpromising basis for the Argument from Design, but at least there would be nothing absurd in such a way of proceeding. On that milder view it is an empirical matter that some people order things in manner X and others in manner Y. But for Kant the case is very different. For Kant it is not an empirical matter that we order our experience by the categories of unity and plurality, cause and effect, and the rest. It is a condition of our experience that things are ordered in this way; there can be no experience otherwise. It is clear that on Kant's principles observation of order in nature cannot be evidence for the existence of a divine orderer; for the reason, putting it crudely (for the Kantian doctrine is a subtle one), that the order

18

we observe is not really out there. It is a product of our observation, rather than an object of it. It is admittedly somewhat misleading to say that Kant believed that order is 'not really out there'; for this could be taken as carrying the suggestion that it might have been there though in fact it happens not to be; or that some people have a kind of *illusion* of order as something actually in nature itself and need to be disabused of it. Kant's view, however, is concerned with how we are to understand the concept of order, rather than with whether order exists or not. That there is order is not really in question. But how is the notion of order to be *understood*? The Kantian view that order is 'mind-imposed' (if we may put that convenient label upon it) is not properly represented by saying that it is the view that order is 'merely' mind-imposed – meaning something like 'illusory', or even 'non-existent'.

I remarked above that the challenge to the Argument from Design implicit in Kant's doctrine is capable of being met. One line that might be taken against Kant has already emerged. Kant's doctrine is a logical doctrine, in the sense that it is a doctrine about the meaning of the notion of order, rather than a doctrine about the presence or absence of order (the *amount* of order in the universe). To the extent that the Argument from Design depends upon claims that the universe exhibits a large amount of order, Kant's doctrine does not directly affect it. But this is merely a partial, and a relatively weak, response to the Kantian challenge; and in any case not all proponents of the Argument have wanted to put much weight upon the claim that there is a large amount of order in the universe; Paley, for instance, although he was at pains to insist on the wide variety and considerable quantity of design in the universe, also said that if necessary a single clear example of design in the universe – that of the eye – would be enough to prove a designer (Paley, p. 46). A stronger response to the Kantian challenge is needed, if it can be found. Such a stronger response would seem to be provided by the following consideration. Kant's doctrine requires a sharp separation between things as they are in themselves and things as we experience them – between the undifferentiated manifold and the categories in terms of which our experience is ordered. But there is an incoherence in this notion of a sharp separation between the world as it is in itself, unexperienced, and the concepts that we bring to our experience of

19

it. How can we talk sensibly of the existence of a world independent of order, when to talk at all is to impose order? It is true that we bring concepts to our experience of the world, but we also acquire them from our experience of the world: there is a kind of two-way traffic here. The Kantian doctrine is a difficult one, and we cannot pursue it further within our present limits. I propose simply to take it that at least the beginnings of an answer to Kant lie in what has just been said, and that if that is so then Kant's doctrine does not set up an insuperable obstacle in the way of proceeding with the discussion of the Argument from Design.

Is Design-B Mind-imposed?

The movement of the arrow towards the target, in Aquinas's analogy, is a case of something happening in accordance with the intention, or purpose, of the archer. Suppose, however, to go back to a point made earlier, that an onlooker thinks he detects in someone's behaviour a purpose that is not the purpose of the agent but something the agent never intended. Suppose, even, that an onlooker detects in someone's behaviour a purpose where in fact no purpose was in his mind (that is, as some would put it, where he was not *acting* at all, as the onlooker thought, but where something was happening to him – for example, where a part of his body was moving in a way which the onlooker mistook for a deliberate action but which was merely a physical reflex). Some people are prone to detect sinister intentions where the intentions are in fact innocent: the person smiling at them is being sympathetic over their efforts to put up the tent frame, not laughing at them. Some may see a sinister intention even where there is no intention at all: the person whistling through his teeth while he looks at the view out of the train window is doing it 'unconsciously' and not with the intention of annoying his fellow-passengers.

Thus, when someone claims to be able to detect benevolent purpose in the workings of the universe, is it not possible that he has mistaken for benevolent a purpose that is other than benevolent? Or, indeed, if he claims to be able to detect purpose of any kind, is it not possible that he has mistaken for something like purposive action what is not purposive action at

20

all? That there is no such mistake, it might be said, needs to be shown by the proponents of the Argument. Hence, of course, the attempts that many of them have made to build up a large quantity of 'evidence', drawn from varied sources: they thus seem to be acknowledging that the onus is on them to show that there is no mistake; or in other words to demonstrate, if they can, the strength of the analogy between human purposiveness and what they claim to be divine purposiveness. Human purposiveness we know from the inside; divine purposiveness we need to have shown to us.

Some objections to the Argument consist in developing just these difficulties. The existence of evil in the universe is brought forward as an objection to the Argument (see, on this, Chapter 4). Some of the strongest attacks on the Argument have been directed squarely against the analogy between human purposive action, or its products, and the universe.

I am at present expressing these lines of objection in very general terms: in effect, that people 'only think they see' purpose, or (it may be) a particular kind of purpose, in the universe. It will be clear, however, that specific and serious difficulties for the Argument are involved here, and it is necessary now to consider more closely the whole notion of design-B as used in connection with the universe and its parts. Both in the next chapter, on purpose, and in that which follows it, on analogy, we shall be concerned with matters which bear on the possibility that design-B is mind-imposed: this is not something to which a short answer can be given here.

3 Purpose in the Universe

It is now time to look more closely at the notion of purpose, which is central to the Argument.

Actions and the Products of Action

Purpose is found in actions and in the products of action – in both the actual doing of something and the thing itself once done. The snooker player in the act of striking the ball can be said to be acting with a purpose. The ball's being in such-and-such a position after the stroke is over can be said to be the result of purpose, or to suggest the player's next intention, etc.

In the case of the universe, things happen, or are the case, which the proponent of the Argument sees as divine actions or the products of divine action. He claims that what happens, or much of what happens, does so in accordance with some divine purpose. He claims that what is the case, or much of it, is so because it is the product of some divine action.

To say that purpose can be seen in the products of actions is to say that purpose can be seen in things at rest – that is, in some kinds of things at rest, for it cannot, of course, be seen in all. An arrow embedded in a target suggests purpose to us, whereas a stone on a beach does not. Of course, the arrow may be there as the result of a whirlwind, and the stone may have been placed where it is by someone in order to act as the finishing-mark for a race; but these are not the most natural suppositions, and we should need evidence to the contrary if we were to feel justified in departing from the normal supposition that human purpose was exhibited in the former case and not in the latter. There are certain situations which we normally assume to be the products of human action, and we do not need to be persuaded that they are so. There are others which we normally do not assume to be the products of human action, and we need to be persuaded that they are. The task of persuasion is more difficult the further removed from our common assumptions is the interpretation in question. Suppose we come upon a number of letter-blocks lying on the floor and find that they spell out the first line of one of Shakespeare's sonnets. It would be a highly unreasonable supposition that they had been knocked from the table and had merely happened to fall in that order. We should naturally suppose that someone had arranged them: that their making this kind of sense was the result of purpose or intention on someone's part. A heap of sand in a garden is probably there as the result of someone's purposive action; sand on a beach is probably not. Yet it is possible that a beach is man-made; and it is even possible that the blocks have been knocked down from the table and have happened to fall in such a way as to read 'No longer mourn for me when I am dead'. Possible; but exceedingly unlikely.

Experience and habit decide which things we assume without question, or almost without question, to be the products of purposive action, and which we do not. Equally, they play a large part in deciding precisely what purpose we see in things, assuming we see purpose at all. Hence the force of Paley's point, referred to in Chapter 1, that attention to the Argument from Design helps to implant in a man a *habit of mind* in which evidence of God's designing hand is seen all about him. Those who expect to see something are likely to see it. Conversely, of course, 'none so blind as those that *will not* see'.

On the face of it, it would seem that evidence of purpose ought to be more successfully available in the case of actions than in that of the products of action. If you actually observe someone doing something, there are ways of finding out whether he is acting with intention. But if all you are given is a state of affairs and you have to decide whether or not it is the end-product of purposive action, the difficulty is greater. That we do not in practice have much difficulty with such situations, as far as ordinary human affairs are concerned, is presumably due to the workings of experience and habit, as has just been mentioned. But there does seem to be more of a gap between the interpretation in terms of purpose and what is interpreted in the case of putative products of action than in that of actions themselves.

An important part of the significance of miracles in religious belief is no doubt that they are seen as particularly direct evidence of divine activity. God is seen to be doing something. This is worth more than an argument that some state of affairs or other has come about in accordance with a presumed divine purpose or intention. The primitive tribesman for whom in the thunder and lightning the gods are angry has no need of philosophy to persuade him of the existence of the gods. The gods are acting, and he observes their action. A written account of a miracle cannot have the directness that actual experience of a miracle would have; but even a written account of a miracle may enable one to see (or think one sees) God at work, in a much sharper way than by being persuaded to see something as the end-product of a divine action that has taken place off-stage.

Purpose in the universe one would expect to appear in its purest, most direct, form in the analogue of human action rather than in the analogue of the products of human action. If we knew what a divine purpose looked like we might not have much difficulty in seeing in such-and-such a state of affairs evidence of things being as they are as the result of divine action, or as set up ready to serve as the starting-point of some future divine action. But if we do not know what a divine purpose looks like, it will not be easy to see divine purpose in a static situation. On the level of human affairs we have experience and habit to help us; but as far as God and the universe are concerned we have not: 'we' here meaning the average twentieth-century scientifically-oriented man. The point has commonly been made that it is a mistake to try to base belief in God upon belief in miracles. The proper order of things is the reverse of this: belief in God makes possible belief in miracles. The man who does not already believe in God will probably not even use the concept of miracle. It would be absurd, then, to suggest to a present-day proponent of the Argument from Design that he should make an appeal to miracles in attempting to build up empirical or quasi-empirical evidence for God. In any case, of course, it is not only in miracles that men have claimed to see the hand of God at work in the world. Nevertheless, attempts to prove God

25

through evidence of purpose in the universe would undoubtedly receive help from the possession of a frame of mind in which the universe is naturally seen as a place in which God *does* things – or rather in which things happen that seem to the observer to show clearly the *present activity* of God – as opposed to a frame of mind receptive to evidence of purpose in the sense merely of the (putative) products of purposive activity. But then, of course, all the familiar objections to miracles would become objections to the Argument from Design. Miracles have commonly been taken to be divine interventions in the normal workings of nature. But for the universe to be intelligible it needs to be a law-governed universe, which is what we find it to be. It is not easy to see how some laws might be suspended in an arbitrary way and the universe remain intelligible. In any case, the very notion of a law of nature being 'suspended' seems to argue a misunderstanding of the meaning of 'laws of nature' – as if laws of nature were like regulations which could be created, rescinded, complied with, or broken: they are not that kind of law, so that the very notion of laws of nature being 'suspended' hardly makes sense.

I have suggested that if we are to argue by analogy with human purposiveness we should expect the clearest evidence of a supreme designer of the universe to show itself in the analogue of human action rather than in the analogue of the products of human action; and we have noted the case of miracles as providing such an analogue of human action. Yet in practice, of course, it is not on miracles that the Argument from Design has been based. It is not the unique, the unusual, the inexplicable (I do not mean to suggest that 'unusual or inexplicable event' would be an adequate *definition* of 'miracle') that has been appealed to as evidence of the divine designer. This is perhaps not surprising as far as design-A is concerned; for the notions of order, regularity or pattern go along with that of repetition, and with that of continuity. A single set of circumstances could no doubt exhibit order, regularity, pattern; but we commonly do not understand these notions in relation to single sets of circumstances. Further, order, regularity or pattern we generally take in a sense that involves the notion of spatial and/or temporal continuity. We should probably not say that the solar system exhibited order unless we believed that it had gone on functioning in the same way for untold ages. But it is not so obvious that design-B (which is after all our concern in the present chapter) involves in quite this way the notions of repetition or of spatial and/or temporal continuity. (The distinction between design-A and design-B was explained on p. 8.) It is true that, as we have noted, experience and habit normally tell us when an explanation in terms of purpose is appropriate, and this certainly suggests some kind of continuity; but it is not the case that the set of circumstances that we are concerned with must itself be regarded as extended through time or space. Human actions, unlike the solar system, typically occupy very little time or space. A typical human purposive action is something like the action of a man getting out of his chair and switching on the electric fire. If we are to look for evidence of divine purposive action in the universe after the analogy with human purposive action, it would seem reasonable to look for something relatively brief and pointed. Admittedly, the span of human life is short, so that it is perhaps not to be wondered at that human actions are typically rather brief; whereas divine actions we might reasonably suppose to be rather grander, larger, longer. But how grand, large or long can they be before they would cease to be easily identifiable as actions at all? If the claim to be able to detect divine purpose in the universe *by analogy with human purpose* is taken as referring to purposive action (rather than the products of action), one would expect miracles to be placed well to the fore among the evidence. At the same time, it must be admitted that although divine miracles resemble human purposive actions in the respect that they are, as it were, brief and to the point, they fail to resemble them in another, very important, respect. Miracles are essentially out-of-the-ordinary events; human actions are not. If we are to keep closely to the analogy with human purposive action we should presumably expect to find divine purposive action wearing a rather ordinary, commonplace aspect. (Yet if it did, it would be all too easy to miss it.)

Proponents of the Argument from Design have refrained from appealing to miracles for the reason, no doubt, that they supposed an argument from *design* to need a basis in the regularity, the continuity, of things – as evidencing the continuing purposes or plans of the great divine designer. But this is to put the stress on design-A; and if it is supposed that the same basis is needed when the stress is on design-B, that indicates a failure to appreciate fully the difference between design-A and design-B.

When is it Appropriate to Seek an Explanation in Terms of Purposive Action?

When might someone be justified in thinking – as opposed to his merely being disposed to think – that he has detected purpose in the universe?

It might be supposed that what would chiefly justify this would be the absence of a scientific explanation – in the sense of an explanation in causal terms. It is true that a reason why people have sometimes sought explanations of certain events or states of affairs in terms of divine purpose has been because they could not readily see a scientific explanation. But it would be a mistake to regard explanation in terms of purpose as a replacement or substitute for scientific or causal explanation (or for that matter vice versa). These are explanations of different kinds; they do not answer the same need. It is never inappropriate to go on seeking a causal explanation of anything in nature, however long it may be in coming; and its absence does not indicate that an explanation in terms of divine activity must be offered as the alternative. Causal explanations and explanations in terms of divine purpose are not alternatives to each other. Whether or not a causal explanation is readily to hand has nothing logically to do with whether it is appropriate to seek for an explanation in terms of purpose. (It should be noted that the Argument from Design has been regarded as itself a quasi-scientific argument. See, on this, Chapter 5. 'Scientific explanation' does not always convey exactly the same sense. It will be enough to note that for our purposes in the present chapter it is to be taken as meaning explanation in causal terms.)

It is not the case, as has sometimes been supposed, that the work of Darwin rules out explanation in terms of purpose. The adaptation of means to end in the biological sphere could readily be seen, after Darwin, as the effect of a long period of interaction between species and environment. An animal is not thus and thus in order to be able to survive in its environment; it has survived in that environment because it is thus and thus. One effect of this was to make widely familiar the notion of design without a designer. Darwin's work made it possible to explain in the case of certain things why they are as they are, without the necessity of expressing this explanation in terms of divine purpose. But Darwin did not dispose of the possibility of that kind of explanation, but rather complicated the matter by moving it one stage further away. Indeed, what happened after the Darwinian controversy in religious circles had died down was that liberal theologians began to maintain that 'God works through evolution'. They combined scientific explanation with explanation in terms of purpose. The need to explain living things by invoking God was still met, but it came to be couched not in terms of direct divine creation of species but in terms of indirect divine action through the working of the evolutionary process. (In some respects, indeed, Darwin's view could be said to be more congenial to Christian belief than was the pre-Darwinian Creationist view. On that view, for instance, the palaeontological evidence of whole species being wiped out and replaced by others had to be explained as the direct effect of divine action; Darwin's view, however, removed this destruction of species from at any rate the direct responsibility of God. What has been called 'the colossal waste of the evolutionary process' could now be seen as only the indirect consequence of the Creator's will.)

The mere absence, or apparent absence, of a scientific explanation, then, will not of itself justify having resort to an explanation in terms of purpose. Nevertheless, it is a fact that sometimes we are puzzled not, say, by how something has come about or by how it works, but by what it 'means', by whether there is some intention behind it, or the like. In what sort of circumstances do we experience such puzzlement? Consider the following anecdote, from Paul Janet's *Final Causes*:

A Scottish philosopher, the wise Beattie, formed the ingenious idea of putting in operation the proof of final causes, to inspire his young child with faith in Providence. This child was five or six years old, and was beginning to read; but his father had not yet sought to speak to him of God, thinking that he was not of an age to understand such lessons. To find entrance into his mind for this great idea in a manner suitable to his age, he thought of the following expedient. In a corner of a little garden, without telling any one of the circumstance,

29

he drew with his finger on the earth the three initial letters of his child's name, and, sowing garden cresses in the furrows, covered the seed and smoothed the earth. 'Ten days after,' he tells us, 'the child came running to me all amazed, and told me that his name had grown in the garden. I smiled at these words, and appeared not to attach much importance to what he had said. But he insisted on taking me to see what had happened. "Yes," said I, on coming to the place, "I see well enough that it is so; but there is nothing wonderful in this, – it is a mere accident," and went away. But he followed me, and, walking beside me, said very seriously: "That cannot be an accident. Some one must have prepared the seeds, to produce this result." Perhaps these were not his very words, but this was the substance of his thought. "You think, then," said I to him, "that what here appears as regular as the letters of your name, cannot be the product of chance?" "Yes," said he firmly, "I think so." "Well, then, look at yourself, consider your hands and fingers, your legs and feet, and all your members, and do they not seem to you regular in their appearance, and useful in their service? Doubtless they do. Can they, then, be the result of chance?" "No," replied he, "that cannot be; some one must have made me them." "And who is that some one?" I asked him. He replied that he did not know. I then made known to him the name of the great Being who made all the world, and regarding His nature I gave him all the instruction that could be adapted to his age. The lesson struck him profoundly, and he has never forgotten either it or the circumstance that was the occasion of it.' (Janet, pp. 292–3)

Beattie's son was justified in seeking an explanation other than one in scientific terms for this phenomenon. We may suppose him familiar with the process of germination of seeds – in the sense at least of being familiar with the activity of putting seeds into the ground and finding flowers, etc., grow in that place. What required explanation was not that the cress grew but that the letters of his name appeared on the ground. How was this? What did it mean? Why not his mother's name? Why anyone's name? What was clear to the boy, according to the story, was that this was no 'accident'; someone had done it. This, indeed, was the aim behind the whole thing. The message intended to be drawn from it was, initially at any rate, simply that someone had engineered this phenomenon. It was natural for the boy to seek for an explanation in terms of purpose.

In this instance, then, neither a scientific explanation nor an explanation in terms of chance seems adequate. This strikes the boy with no help from anyone. He does, however, have to be helped to see that the same might be said about the workings of his hands and fingers, legs and feet. Beattie – and he is not alone among supporters of the Argument from Design in this – offers the boy explicitly only a choice between design by someone and mere chance. The choice ought, however, to involve three items: explanation in scientific terms, 'explanation' in terms of chance (which by comparison with the other two is no explanation at all), and explanation in terms of purpose. The second of these is incompatible with either of the others; but the others, as we have noted already, are compatible with each other. The analogy the father is implying between his own designing of the appearance of the boy's name on the ground and God's designing of the parts of the boy's body is an imperfect one. The growing of cress and the workings of human hands or feet are both subjects of scientific investigation. But *the name spelt in cress* is a unique event, whereas the boy is one boy among many. What is striking about the appearance of the boy's name on the ground is its unique reference to him: it is natural to see the choice here as lying between mere chance and someone's purpose, and purpose wins hands down. But in the case of the workings of his body (because the boy's body is like multitudes of other bodies) the choice lies more naturally between being content with a scientific explanation and demanding in addition one in terms of purpose. The need for explanation in terms of purpose is, however, by no means as striking as in the case of the name on the ground. The situation does not seem to demand a choice between mere chance and divine purpose. This would be to assume that a question like 'What does it mean?' is an appropriate one to ask. But prior to that choice – which is the choice Beattie offers – there is a more fundamental one: whether or not to ask such a question at all. To ask it probably implies some kind of hope that 'life has a meaning', or the like; so an answer in terms of purpose is pretty well ensured. There is a shift in Beattie's procedure from a case where such a question seems clearly in place (the name in cress) to a

31

case where it is less obviously in place (the workings of the boy's body).

One possible answer to the question of when it is appropriate to look for an explanation of something in nature in terms of purpose is suggested by the anecdote about Beattie and his son. We are justified in looking for an explanation of some natural event in terms of purpose in cases where there is some element of uniqueness or of personal reference. (Compare what was said above about miracles.) But this is only part of the answer. Traditionally, as we remarked earlier, it is regularities rather than uniquenesses in nature that the proponents of the Argument from Design have appealed to; and this would suggest an answer to the question that is virtually the opposite of the one that emerges from the anecdote about Beattie and his son. Further, complexity has sometimes been thought to be important here. That is, it has been supposed that the more complex, or apparently complex, the workings of some natural phenomenon – say, the human eye or ear – the more need there is to invoke a divine designer. There are historical reasons for the Argument's being based on regularities in nature (design-A). In its heyday in the eighteenth and nineteenth centuries the Argument achieved a form that was intended to be as far as possible scientifically respectable. The influence of Newton was important in this (see Hurlbutt).

Of course, it is always permissible to look for an explanation of anything in nature in terms of purpose; just as it is always permissible to look for an explanation of anything in nature in scientific terms. What I have been concerned with is the question of whether there are times when it is more appropriate or more natural to do so than at others. It seems to me that to someone who is not predisposed to believe in a divine designer of the universe, it is a natural phenomenon unique in character or having special reference to himself that might be most likely to strike him as needing explanation in terms of purpose; this is what the Beattie anecdote brings out. It is true that the unique event mentioned in that anecdote – the name in cress – was brought about by Beattie, not by God. But the parallel with miracles is clear. The somewhat surprising thing is that Beattie, having attracted the boy's interest by the name on the ground, did not go on to draw an analogy with miraculous events that could be seen to need the same sort of explanation – an explanation in terms of (divine) purpose. He went on in fact to talk about entirely regular and orderly happenings, like the workings of people's hands and feet. There is no indication in the story that it was in any sense the extraordinary character, or the complexity of the workings, of hands and feet that he wanted to call to the boy's attention; rather it was the regularity of their working, and their usefulness. The name on the ground had the effect of gaining the boy's attention; but thereafter no use seems to have been made by Beattie of the special character of that event. He might as well have simply started with the regularity and usefulness of hands and feet. Admittedly, someone who (like Beattie's son, if we are to believe the story) has not had any religious teaching will hardly have the concept of miracle, and there will therefore be difficulties in introducing him to the notion of divine purposive action through the explanation of certain events as miracles; yet this would seem to be the logical direction in which to proceed. If not, what is the point of such a beginning as Beattie provided? I suggest, then, that in the case of someone who is not predisposed to believe in a divine designer, the kind of thing that it might seem appropriate to seek an explanation for in terms of (divine) purpose is the unique, the unusual; for example, that which surprisingly seems to have a personal reference to oneself. Now, in the case of someone who is predisposed to believe in a divine designer, the unusual – in the shape of miracles – will also, naturally, seem an appropriate field in which to search for support for the belief in a divine purposing mind. But someone predisposed to such belief is likely to consider that the order and regularity of the universe offers an even more appropriate field. Perhaps Beattie (not unnaturally, being himself a believer) followed a kind of reasoning with his son that was more appropriate to himself than to the boy, and failed to put to its best use – at any rate its most natural use – the ingeniously contrived event from which he started.

A final word on the question: When is it appropriate to look for an explanation of natural events in terms of purpose? The answer that the proponent of the Argument from Design himself would probably be most likely to give is that it is appropriate to look for such an explanation when, or to the extent that, we are struck by the way in which the universe is analogous to a machine or a number of machines (machines have designers).

33

But to have been struck by the likeness of the universe, or parts of it, to machines, is already to have decided that it is appropriate to look for an explanation of natural events in terms of purpose. The examination of the analogy with machines, and related topics, lies at the centre of the Argument from Design, and we shall be taking this up in the next chapter. The present discussion is preliminary to that.

Two Kinds of Design-B

It is claimed in the Argument from Design that the universe exhibits design-B. This is to be interpreted, at any rate initially, as meaning that different parts, or different aspects, of the universe exhibit design-B, rather than that the universe-as-a-whole exhibits design-B, in the sense that there is such a thing as '*the* meaning of the universe', i.e. that there is some single design behind the whole. The Argument is based on supposed empirical evidence of design, and it is implausible that there should be initially empirical evidence of a single design in terms of which the whole universe is to be explained; this is something that would need to be worked up to through the production of particular pieces of evidence.

These particular pieces of evidence may not all be of the same kind. There is no one sense in which different parts or aspects of the universe may be said all to exhibit design-B. The difference between animate and inanimate things is important here; further, among animate things, the difference between rational and non-rational is important, and among inanimate things that between natural things and artefacts. To take artefacts first: these are said to *serve* a purpose – not their own, of course, but a purpose of human beings. Natural things may also serve a purpose (as a depression in the rock-face serves as a foothold for the mountaineer), but we do not – unless, indeed, we are under the influence of the Argument from Design – say that they were *made* to serve a purpose. Where there is change or movement in artefacts we may speak of this change as having some purpose: the pistons move up and down in the cylinders so that eventually the wheels of the car may move along the road. We may or may not refer to this as a means/end relationship. It is natural to say that the engine – or, indeed, the whole car of which it is a

34

part – is made to function in order that its owner may get about quickly and conveniently from place to place; it is the means to that end. But of the parts of the engine, or of the car, in relation to each other, we should probably not normally, I think, use the language of means/end; we might more naturally talk of purpose – ultimately, of course, we should be implying the purpose of the artificer. Of natural things we should not often talk either in terms of 'means/end' or of 'purpose'. Again, though we should not, I think, *normally* do this, the object of the Argument from Design is to get us to do so.

Where animate things are concerned there is more scope for the notion of purpose. Although some of the proponents of the Argument from Design have drawn their evidence from the inanimate world, it has seemed to others that the best evidence will be that which comes from the animate world. As Paley remarked: 'My opinion of Astronomy has always been, that it is *not* the best medium through which to prove the agency of an intelligent Creator; but that, this being proved, it shews, beyond all other sciences, the magnificence of his operations' (Paley, p. 223).

There are a number of expressions that we use of human actions – such as 'rational', 'intentional', done from such-and-such a 'motive', done with such-and-such a 'purpose', done 'for the sake of' such-and-such. An attempt to detect the hand of God in the universe involves the detection not simply of divine 'purpose' strictly so called; terminological changes can be rung on the notions of divine intention or divine motive, or divine action for the sake of such-and-such an end, etc. Quite apart from human action, there is in the case of organisms (including human organisms), as in the case of machines, movement or change that may call for explanation in terms of 'design': the heart pumps blood in order to distribute oxygen to distant parts of the body. A human organism's workings can be described after the analogy of a machine, or in some cases of an electrical system.

There is no need to elaborate further on the diversity that exists among the meanings of the notion of design-B. The question that concerns us is how this diversity affects the Argument from Design. The issue can be simplified as follows. There are importantly two kinds of design-B to be considered. First, there is design-B as this is exhibited on the level of

35

inanimate things or on the level of organisms considered as functioning mechanically; let us call this design-B1. Secondly, there is design-B as this is exhibited in human purposive action; let us call this design-B2.

Now, no proponent of the Argument, as far as I know, has taken design-B2 as the starting-point of his argument. The reason presumably is that this kind of design intuitively seems self-explanatory. If the assumption is that purpose needs to be explained in terms of a purposing agent, then in human purposive action we have purpose of a kind where the purposing agent is clearly present and identifiable. The Argument from Design, involving as it does the drawing of an *analogy* between a human architect and the divine architect, naturally looks for the latter only in places where the former is not clearly visible at work. If you are depending on an analogy between X and Y, you do not want to invoke both X and Y at the same time to explain the same things: to explain one situation *by analogy with* another is not to explain both situations in the *same* way. The movement of the arrow to the target is explained adequately by invoking the archer: it is when there are no archers to be seen that we may want to invoke an invisible divine archer.

At any rate, the assumption does seem to be that design-B2 is self-sufficient but that design-B1 is not. Design-B2, being self-sufficient, can then be appealed to to provide an analogical basis or explanation or justification for design-B1. One is reminded of certain views about deductive and inductive inference. Deductive inference, being assumed not to be in need of justification, has been called in by some philosophers to provide a justification of inductive inference, which is supposed not to be self-sufficient. An assumption behind the Argument from Design, somewhat similarly, may be that design-B2 is something that needs no justification, whereas design-B1 is incomplete, in need of justification; and that the former can conveniently provide the justification that the latter needs. Evidence of design-B1 suggests the need for an explanation in terms of design-B2, or something like it. A watch needs to be explained in terms of someone's intentions, but those intentions themselves, it is assumed, need only to be stated, and do not call for further explanation. Equally, the human eye needs to be explained in terms of someone's intentions – namely, God's – and such an explanation is finally satisfying.

36

Suppose someone did attempt to argue to God from design-B2; that is, suppose he tried to build up an argument on the assumption that human purposive action is not self-explanatory but needs to be explained in terms of another purpose beyond itself. (As if someone were to say that deduction as much as induction needs to be justified in terms of some notion of inference more fundamental than either of them.) This more ultimate purpose is – at any rate this is what we may suppose will then be argued – a divine purpose. The true final explanation of human purposive action would be that it is something brought about in accordance with God's purposes rather than itself a bringing about of something in accordance with the agent's purposes. Indeed, the 'agent' would hardly be an agent at all. He might think that he was acting deliberately, or with intention, etc.; in reality, he would be acting in accordance with someone else's (God's) intentions. For our purposes, the important point here is not whether this is a correct or an incorrect view of what we normally call human purposive action, but simply that if this account were adopted it would gravely weaken the distinction between design-B2 and design-B1. A case of design-B2 would be 'really' the effect or result of purposive action rather than itself purposive action; and consequently it would be closely akin to design-B1. But from the point of view of the Argument from Design it will not do to weaken in this way the distinction between design-B1 and design-B2. Design-B2 is needed in all its strength and independence and self-sufficiency alongside design-B1. Otherwise design-B1 cannot be explained in terms of design-B2. The analogy which is to be drawn between the human purposing agent and the divine architect depends for its effectiveness on its being possible to give a clear meaning to design-B2. If explanation in terms of the purposes of independent human agents is not largely self-sufficient, then there are serious difficulties for the Argument from Design. The analogy between human agent and divine architect cannot begin unless we are able to isolate the concept of human purposing agent from other aspects of purpose. It is not possible to argue from design-B1 to God as divine architect unless we already have the notion of design-B2, which would be, of course, exemplified in the actions of a divine architect but which we must have acquired already through our knowledge of human agents if there is to be any sense in the *analogy* on which the Argument

37

from Design depends. (According to 'mechanism', human purposes and intentions are epiphenomenal; on this view human purposive action is in fact not, as we have been saying, independent and self-sufficient but to be explained in causal or 'mechanistic' terms. See Chapter 6. For arguments against mechanism see Malcolm [1] and [2].)

In short, it is not possible to construct an Argument from Design which finds its evidence of design purely in the form of design-B2. And I do not think it would be advisable for proponents of the Argument even to include evidence of design-B2 along with evidence of design-B1. Design-B2 belongs in the explanation, not with what is to be explained.

It is clear, then, that the Argument from Design-B must be an argument from design-B1. So, indeed, we find it to be; but the foregoing will have explained why this is, and must be, so.

Can there be Design-B1 without a Designer?

Although it is possible to give a complete account of the workings of, say, a watch, without referring to the fact that the watch is an artefact, it is not possible to give a complete account of the watch itself (as opposed to an account of its workings) without such reference. Supposing all reference to the fact that a watch was something made to serve a purpose to be omitted, the account of the watch would lack something. Equally, if it is the case that the universe, or parts of it, had a designer, then an account of the universe (as opposed to an account of its workings) that omitted reference to this could also be said to lack something.

An important difference between a watch and the universe lies in the fact that we *know* a watch to be something designed, and intended to fulfil the design of the watchmaker, and it is because we know this that we can see that an account of a watch that omitted reference to such things would be incomplete. If in the case of the universe we knew, or believed, that it was fulfilling the designs of God, then we could similarly see that an account of it that omitted all reference to this would be incomplete. On Paley's interpretation of the Argument from Design this is in fact the situation: we approach the universe looking for evidence of the divine designer in whom we already

38

believe. But if the Argument from Design is interpreted as an argument to the existence of God which does not depend on prior belief in God, the position is not so straightforward. What is it in our examination of the universe that could justify us in saying that an account of it which omitted reference to a divine designer would be incomplete?

Professor Charles Taylor, in his *The Explanation of Behaviour*, discusses among other things the question whether a teleological explanation requires reference to purpose as an 'unobservable entity'. It is an assumption of what Taylor calls 'atomism' (which seeks to reduce teleological explanation to non-teleological) that teleological explanation involves the postulation of purpose in the sense of a non-observable entity. Atomism rejects such an entity and claims in so doing to have disposed of teleological explanation. Taylor, however, maintains that it is a mistake to suppose that teleological explanation necessarily involves the postulation of purpose as a non-observable entity. The denial of such an entity, therefore, does not dispose of teleological explanation. Taylor's book is not concerned with the Argument from Design, but the arguments of atomists (as Taylor represents them) against purpose in the sense of a non-observable entity, and also the arguments of Taylor against atomism itself, are relevant to the Argument. From the point of view of the atomists (whose view we may generalise into the form: a purely non-teleological explanation of the universe – one which dispenses with the notion of purpose – is all that is needed to provide a complete account of it), the attempt of the Argument from Design to introduce explanation in terms of God's purposes faces an extremely uphill task. But, equally, if Taylor is right as against the atomists, the Argument from Design is still not helped; for Taylor, though he makes use of teleological explanation, understands it in a way which, as much as does the atomists' non-teleological explanation, dispenses with the need for purpose as an entity and makes systems appear self-explanatory.

Taylor writes: '. . . to explain by purpose is to explain by the goal or result aimed at, "for the sake of" which the event is said to occur' (Taylor, pp. 5–6).

Now the fact that the state of a system and its environment is such as to require a given event if a certain result is to accrue

39

can be perfectly observable, and the fact that this antecedent condition holds can be established independently of the evidence provided by the occurrence of the event itself. . . . The element of 'purposiveness' in a given system, the inherent tendency towards a certain end, which is conveyed by saying that the events happen 'for the sake of' the end, cannot be identified as a special entity which directs the behaviour from within, but consists rather in the fact that in beings with a purpose an event's being required for a given end is a sufficient condition of its occurrence. It is not a separable feature, but a property of the whole system, that by which it tends 'naturally' towards a certain result or end. (Taylor, p. 10)

This account of purpose, as we see, dispenses with the notion of purpose as 'a separate entity which is the cause or antecedent' (Taylor, p. 7) of some piece of behaviour. This account, according to which purpose is a property of a whole system and not a separable entity, is clearly uncongenial to the traditional Argument from Design. If the presence of purpose in a system meant that there is a kind of separable 'cause or antecedent', the step to explanation in terms of a purposing mind might well seem not too difficult a one to take. But if purpose in a system means merely that in that system events happen for the sake of an end, *and that this is simply a feature of the system itself as a whole*, the step to explanation in terms of a purposing *mind* is less easy. In the terminology I am using, design-B1 would be self-explanatory and not in need of explanation in terms of design-B2.

There are two comments that I wish to make on Taylor's position, which, it seems to me, turns out on examination not to raise so serious a difficulty for the Argument from Design as undoubtedly appears at first sight. In the first place, a teleological explanation, as Taylor presents it, seems to function as an explanation of elements within a system rather than of a system itself. As far as the system itself is concerned it seems to function more as a description than as an explanation. We explain why event E happens by saying that it happens 'for the sake of' goal G. But of the whole system S of which E and G are elements we say that it is a teleological system, and this does not explain it but rather describes or classifies it. This would seem to leave the way open for *explanation* of the whole system, which might

40

be in terms of design-B2. In the second place, as we have noted, an account of a watch that omitted all reference to its having had a designer would be in a fairly obvious sense incomplete. In the case of the universe, or parts of it, there is always the possibility of asking for an explanation in terms of design-B2. How far we are justified in pressing for such an explanation must depend on the arguments drawn from *analogy* on which the Argument from Design essentially depends, and which we are to examine in the following chapter. Even although an account, like that of Taylor, were to be given on which design-B1 does not point to a necessary explanation in terms of design-B2, we might want to argue that the universe is so very like a watch, or something of the sort, that we are still driven to explain it ultimately in terms of the activity of a designing mind if we are not to rest in an incomplete explanation. Even if we grant the implications of Taylor's position, that there is no direct road from design-B1 to design-B2 (because, on this view, design-B1 is not seen as necessarily incomplete and as requiring completion by design-B2, but, on the contrary, as intelligible on its own), there still remains a not so direct road: the road of analogy.

4 Analogy

Some of the most serious objections that the Argument from Design has had to meet – in particular, those made by Hume in his *Dialogues concerning Natural Religion* – have been directed at its character as an analogical argument. In the present chapter I consider some of the chief difficulties that arise, or have been thought to arise, in this connection.

Finite Effects Suggest Finite Causes

'*Like effects prove like causes*', says Philo in Hume's *Dialogues* (Hume [1] p. 165). And a little later: '. . . as the cause ought only to be proportioned to the effect, and the effect, so far as it falls under our cognisance, is not infinite; what pretensions have we . . . to ascribe that attribute to the divine Being?' (Hume [1] p. 166). Or as Hume says in his *Enquiry*: 'If the cause be known only by the effect, we never ought to ascribe to it any qualities, beyond what are precisely requisite to produce the effect' (Hume [2] p. 136).

The following passages illustrate applications of what is fundamentally the same objection:

> A great number of men join in building a house or a ship, in rearing a city, in framing a commonwealth: Why may not several Deities combine in contriving and framing a world? (Hume [1] p. 167)
> And why not become a perfect anthropomorphite? Why not assert the Deity or Deities to be corporeal, and to have eyes, a nose, mouth, ears, &c.? Epicurus maintained, that no man had ever seen reason but in a human figure; therefore the gods must have a human figure. And this argument, which is deservedly so much ridiculed by Cicero, becomes, according to you, solid and philosophical. (Hume [1] p. 168)

43

Further, for all the advocate of the analogy with human design and human designers knows, it may be that the world

> is very faulty and imperfect, compared to a superior standard; and was only the first rude essay of some infant Deity, who afterwards abandoned it, ashamed of his lame performance; it is the work only of some dependent, inferior Deity; and is the object of derision to his superiors: it is the production of old age and dotage in some superannuated Deity; and ever since his death, has run on at adventures, from the first impulse and active force, which it received from him. (Hume [1] p. 169)

In short, if we are to argue from evidence of design in the universe, we can only argue, at best, to something capable of being responsible for the design we actually observe, but not to anything beyond that. Analogy with design on the human level is capable of suggesting to us something like a number of separate, perhaps even embodied, rational agents with super-human, but still finite, powers. It cannot lead us to *God* – the unique, infinite, perfect God. 'Like effects prove like causes.'

I now proceed to comment on these points. As far as a possible plurality of designers is concerned, a defender of the Argument might suggest that the various parts of the universe in which design can be detected all work together, or all fit into a single harmonious pattern, or all indicate the presence of the same single purpose, and that this is a reason for supposing them after all to be the work of a single designer. But the empirical point of view adopted by the proponents of the Argument is not encouraging to this way of thinking. Is it really the case that observation reveals to us (as opposed to speculation suggesting to us) that the structure of the human eye, and that of the solar system, and that of geological strata, all fit into a single inter-related whole or serve a single purpose? What purpose? Even an Absolute Idealist view, which would be much more accommodating to an argument in support of a single designer, would seem to allow for the possibility of a committee of designers. The proponents of the Argument from Design are in any case most unlikely to be Absolute Idealists; and Hume is fighting the Argument with its own weapons.

On the wider issue, as expressed by Hume in the quotation from the *Enquiry*, that from an effect we can argue only to a cause with qualities adequate to produce just that effect but no more, Professor Swinburne remarks against Hume: 'Any scientist who told us only that the cause of E had E-producing characteristics would not add an iota to our knowledge. Explanation of matters of fact consists in postulating on reasonable grounds that the cause of an effect has certain characteristics other than those sufficient to produce the effect' (Swinburne, p. 207; see also Flew [2] p. 225). This, however, would not meet Hume's specific point in the *Dialogues* that the proponent of the Argument from Design cannot legitimately argue from finite observable things to an infinite, perfect, unique cause. Although the cause might reasonably be held to have characteristics other than those sufficient to produce the effect, it cannot reasonably be held, on the evidence only of the effect, to have the characteristic of being infinite. For Hume (as for Kant later) it was a fault in proponents of the Argument from Design that they supposed themselves to have proved something much closer to the Christian God than they had any right to suppose.

Behind Hume's whole approach to this matter lies his empiricist analysis of causation, according to which knowledge of causes is basically knowledge of things that are capable of being objects of human experience. In order for us to be able to say that A is the cause of B we must, in general, be able to identify both A and B and have had experience of their constant conjunction. Hume's empiricist principles are inhospitable to any argument to the unique, infinite, perfect (and unobservable) God as cause. The most we could say is that 'the cause or causes of order in the universe probably bear some remote analogy to human intelligence' (Hume [1] p. 227).

Swinburne makes the point that argument to unobserved and unobservable causes is, despite Hume, not only possible but an entirely respectable procedure in science. '[A] more developed science than Hume knew has taught us that when observed As have a relation R to observed Bs, it is often perfectly reasonable to postulate that observed A*s, similar to As have the same relation to unobserved and unobservable B*s similar to Bs' (Swinburne, p. 208). Swinburne had earlier given the following example of a scientific argument:

Certain pressures (As) on the walls of containers are produced by billiard balls (Bs) with certain motions. Similar pressures

(A*s) are produced on the walls of containers which contain not billiard balls but gases. Therefore, since we have no better explanation of the existence of the pressures, gases consist of particles (B*s) similar to billiard balls except in certain respects – e.g. size. (Swinburne, p. 205)

Swinburne has shown that scientists in fact argue in ways in which, according to Hume, they probably ought not to argue. But to explain the behaviour of gases by saying that gases are made up of particles is not altogether parallel to explaining that or some other natural phenomenon in terms of the purposes of a divine rational agent. (I am not, of course, suggesting that Swinburne supposes it is.) Both explanations involve postulating unobservables. But the former is still an explanation in recognisably scientific terms – an explanation in terms of physical causes. The latter is not. An explanation in terms of the action of particles is a different kind of explanation from one in terms of the activity of a divine rational agent. Hume was mistaken in denying the possibility of explanation in terms of unobservable causes (at least, this is the tendency of his thought), but it would not follow from considerations about what is permissible in science that one could argue from observation of the physical universe to explanation in terms of a rational agent. Even an Argument from Design-A is not entirely parallel to a scientific argument such as the one about gases. An Argument from Design-B is much less so: a question to which the answer is in terms of divine purposes is a different kind of question from one to which the answer is in terms of the movement of particles.

Hume was wrong to suppose that from our observation of the universe we could never argue to unobservable causes. As Swinburne has made clear, this can be done; for scientists sometimes do it. But Hume's chief point remains: that from finite effects we can argue only to finite causes. At best the Argument from Design can suggest to us the operation of a demiurge. There can be no question of its proving the Christian God, or anything like the Christian God; and this is what Hume was concerned to stress.

At the same time, and by way of a limited kind of defence of the Argument, it is relevant to note that it has commonly gone about in the company of other theistic arguments, and many

46

philosophers have assumed that in any case it cannot be expected to perform unaided the task of proving God. There is perhaps some unfairness in the criticism that the Argument cannot possibly prove the infinite God. Perhaps its function should be regarded as being only that of providing a preparation for other arguments that may have some hope of leading to more profound conclusions – the Cosmological Argument and the Moral Argument, perhaps. It proves something; it must not be expected to prove everything. But Hume's rejoinder to this would no doubt be that if the Argument from Design is not to be expected to carry alone the burden of proof, then neither should the objection to it that we have so far in this chapter been considering be expected to carry alone the burden of disproof; and, certainly, the number of objections that have been made to the theistic arguments greatly exceeds the number of those arguments.

It may be that Hume himself is expecting too much of the Argument. He says that we cannot from finite effects prove any more than a finite cause. But is the Argument from Design setting out to prove a cause at all – whether finite or infinite? Admittedly, it is numbered among the standard or traditional theistic 'proofs'; it is generally taken to be an attempted proof of the existence of God. But at best it proves a designer; and what a designer 'causes' is design in the material he is working with; he is not expected to 'cause' or create the material itself. The sense in which a designer causes is a limited one. By analogy, then, the most we might be expected to be able to show through the Argument from Design is the existence of a super-designer or super-architect, imposing design upon material which already exists. It might be said that this is just what Hume does say about the Argument from Design. But this is not entirely so. To say that we cannot expect to be able to argue from finite effects to anything more than finite causes is still to speak as though the Argument from Design was an argument to a cause or causes, albeit finite and not infinite. If we are to draw limits to what the Argument can reasonably be thought to achieve, the limits can be drawn more narrowly than this. The Argument is not an argument to a cause but to a designer. The less we expect of it, no doubt the less scope there is for it to fall short of expectation.

One type of objection that the Argument from Design has frequently had to meet is that the universe seems to exhibit not only design but the absence of design, the opposite of design, or the presence of evil.

(1) Let us first consider the objection that the universe exhibits absence of design, and let us begin by taking 'design' to mean 'design-A'.

To have experience at all is to have ordered experience (as Kant saw); otherwise we could not say what our experience was experience of. We could not have experience of a totally un-ordered universe. The sense therefore in which we can be said to experience absence of design-A is where this is a limited or relative absence – an absence of order seen against a back-ground of the presence of order. If books are piled up higgledy-piggledy, we can imagine them arranged neatly by authors, or subject-matter, or size. Now what corresponds to this higgledy-pigglediness in our experience of things in nature? We can hardly say that things are lacking in order unless we have in mind some idea of how they would be if they were orderly. Are mountains lacking in order because they are scattered about the surface of the earth somewhat irregularly and are of different heights and composition? Is the solar system lacking in order because the planets are not equidistant from each other? It is unclear what would be the point of a complaint that such things lacked order, or what would be the point of claiming that we could imagine them arranged in ways that were more orderly. What are our standards here? To suppose that things did not happen in regular ways at all, or that things happened without any causes, would be to give up doing science. It is easier to imagine in a given case that some different pattern of regularity, or some other cause, applies, than that no regularity or no cause applies. The objection to the Argument from Design that says that the universe exhibits not only design-A but the *absence* of design-A is not an easy one to understand.

Let us now consider design-B. By contrast with the claim that the universe exhibits absence of design-A, the claim that it exhibits absence of design-B is entirely intelligible. Not every-thing that happens is susceptible of interpretation in terms of

48

means/end; and not everything suggests explanation in terms of purpose or related notions. Nevertheless, this does not seem to constitute a serious objection to the Argument from Design. In order for the hand of a designer to be detected in the universe it is necessary only for it to be fairly easily detectable in some parts of the universe; it is not necessary for it to be detectable in all: if our familiarity with the universe were greater we might expect to detect it more widely, but a little is enough. As Paley said, consideration of the human eye alone should be sufficient to prove a designer.

(2) The objection that the universe exhibits not absence of design but the opposite of design makes a positive and not a negative claim. At least, so it would appear. But what exactly is being claimed? What is the opposite of design? We may take this to be, as opposed to mere lack of order, a state of positive disorder – perhaps like the condition of one's belongings after a burglar has gone through them. Things are said to be reduced to a state of disorder or (more strongly) to a state of chaos; or, from disorder or chaos, order is said to emerge or be created. Here again, if we take the case of design-A, we need to have some notion of what would constitute order and disorder in connection with a particular subject-matter. In the case of design-B (unlike the situation discussed under (1)), there seems to be a difficulty of understanding. Mere absence of purpose is one thing. The existence of what we might call anti-purpose is another, and something altogether more difficult to understand. One sense that might be given to the claim that the universe exhibits the opposite of design is that it exhibits evidence of evil. Advocates of the Argument from Design sometimes tend to suppose that the detection of purpose in the universe means the detection of benevolent purpose. What is being sought, after all, is evidence that will support belief in God, and evidence of a malevolent purpose at work does not help towards that end. Yet purposes and intentions can be bad as well as good. If there is evidence of bad purposes in the universe it is certainly relevant to the issue of the existence of God (if 'God is good' is held to be necessarily true), or at any rate to the issue of the character Christians ascribe to God (if 'God is good' is held to be only contingently true). The adaptation of means to ends in animals, it is sometimes assumed, always works to their preservation, and thus may be taken as evidence of a (good) designer. But this

means/end relation can be of a different kind. If we are to talk in terms of means/end at all we must presumably be prepared to say that a cancer is adapted to kill the organism, not to preserve it: this ought to be taken equally with the other as evidence of design. In short, there is sometimes a tendency to suppose that evidence of design-B must take the form of evidence of benevolent design-B; and what the sceptic might label as evidence of malevolent design-B is simply not seen by the believer as evidence of design at all. But let us now proceed to a fuller discussion of evidence of evil.

(3) John Stuart Mill writes:

> If there are any marks at all of special design in creation, one of the things most evidently designed is that a large proportion of all animals should pass their existence in tormenting and devouring other animals. . . . If a tenth part of the pains which have been expended in finding benevolent adaptations in all nature, had been employed in collecting evidence to blacken the character of the Creator, what scope for comment would not have been found in the entire existence of the lower animals, divided, with scarcely an exception, into devourers and devoured, and a prey to a thousand ills from which they are denied the faculties necessary for protecting themselves! If we are not obliged to believe the animal creation to be the work of a demon, it is because we need not suppose it to have been made by a Being of infinite power. (Mill, p. 58)

What is the relevance of 'the problem of evil' to the Argument from Design? Moral evil (that is, the pain and suffering that men cause each other by their selfishness, cruelty and the like) creates less of a difficulty than natural evil (that is, the pain caused by earthquakes, famines, etc.). The religious believer will generally attempt to account for the former by claiming it to be a necessary concomitant of human free will: for men to be able to choose good, he will say, it is a condition that they must be able also to choose evil. Natural evil, however, is not to be explained in this way; it is a feature of the universe not explicable in terms of human wills. If we are to take seriously the analogical approach, we are forced to conclude, the sceptic would claim, either that the presence of natural evil in the universe is evidence against the existence of God, or that it shows that we can conclude only to a deity of limited powers (limited because he is apparently unable to prevent evil), or perhaps that it is positive evidence for the existence of a devil.

The advocate of the Argument has himself taken his stand upon analogy, and his own kind of argument can be turned against him. Admittedly, no analogy can be pressed too far. Analogies are bound to fall short in some respect or other; if they did not they would be something more than analogies. But there is no doubt a temptation for arguers by analogy to select features that suit them; and equally it no doubt seems to a critic reasonable to insist that an analogy be pressed as far as possible – if that happens to suit *him*. If we are to argue by analogy with human designs and human designers, it is relevant to take note of the bad as well as the good. The case of animal suffering, which Mill stresses, is particularly troublesome for the advocate of the Argument from Design. Human pain or suffering caused by natural events – such as long and painful illness, or accidents – is sometimes accounted for as serving the divine purpose of strengthening the sufferer's character; and this is, indeed, a point of view that Mill himself might be expected to have some sympathy with, in the light of his insistence in his ethical writings on the importance of moral and intellectual character or fibre. But this kind of justification cannot be given in the case of animal suffering. This world may be 'the vale of Soul-making', as Keats called it, for us; but Christian believers have not generally wanted to say that it is a vale of soul-making for animals. Perhaps animals do not really suffer physical pain? The lower animals no doubt do not. But, if we are to argue by analogy, it seems more likely that the higher animals suffer than that they do not. Could things have been designed so that animal suffering might have been less? Hume has something to say on this. He identifies four circumstances upon which natural evil depends, and suggests in each case a better way of arranging things.

(i) The first circumstance is pain (see Hume [1] pp. 205–6). It will be argued that pain plays a part in self-preservation. But pain, says Hume, does not seem necessary for this purpose. Pleasure would do equally well; a feeling of diminution of pleasure could function just as satisfactorily as a feeling of pain in prompting creatures to whatever is necessary to secure their preservation.

(ii) The second circumstance is the fact that the universe seems to work according to inflexible general laws. If you lose your footing on a mountainside, gravity will see to it that your brains are dashed out at the foot. Drink a deadly poison by mistake and unless an antidote is interposed death follows inevitably. Why could not the deity intervene – at least occasionally? Even a few small interventions might have great effects. 'Some small touches, given to Caligula's brain in his infancy, might have converted him into a Trajan: One wave, a little higher than the rest, by burying Caesar and his fortune in the bottom of the ocean, might have restored liberty to a considerable part of mankind' (Hume [1] p. 207). There are doubtless difficulties in the supposition that the deity might *constantly* intervene – that the whole universe might be conducted according to 'particular volitions' rather than general laws – but we need not suppose such an extreme situation. A limited amount of interference is enough. Hume, a little oddly, supposes that this might be done in such a way that we should not detect that particular volitions were being made. (What is odd is the implication that such secrecy on the part of the deity would be a virtue; in fact, it could not help the Argument from Design, which relies upon *evidence*.) One possible comment on this would be that for all we know the deity is already directing things so that their outcome is more favourable for mankind than it would otherwise have been; but Hume's counter might well be that the deity could do still more. Hume might have said in this connection, but does not (though he makes a related point in connection with the third circumstance), that we expect a human designer to be prepared to bend regulations from time to time, if the consequence of not bending them is that harm is caused to someone; and the failure to find evidence of such bending must operate as a consideration against the analogy with human design and a human designer.

(iii) The third circumstance is the frugality with which the deity, if there is one, has distributed to beings their powers. 'Every animal has the requisite endowments; but these endowments are bestowed with so scrupulous an economy, that any considerable diminution must entirely destroy the creature' (Hume [1] p. 207). It would have been better if the deity had created fewer species of animals and 'endowed these with more faculties for their happiness and preservation' (Hume [1] p.

208). Again, however, we might counter Hume's argument by suggesting that for all we know he has already done this. Hume's arguments depend on the suppositions that it is meaningful to imagine the universe as other than it is and (oddly) that it is possible that the deity might manipulate things in such a way that we should, while enjoying the conditions he has brought about, not be aware that they are the result of his particular volitions. My comments on Hume do not question these suppositions; they are limited to suggesting that on his own suppositions Hume's objections are not as strong as they might seem. As far as the present point is concerned, we may say that there is nothing to rule out the possibility that the universe does contain fewer species than it might have contained.

(iv) Even if we are prepared to grant that the parts of the universe serve some purpose, yet often things seem to go wrong.

> Thus, the winds are requisite to convey the vapours along the surface of the globe, and to assist men in navigation: but how oft, rising up to tempests and hurricanes, do they become pernicious? . . . There is nothing so advantageous in the universe, but what frequently becomes pernicious, by its excess or defect; nor has nature guarded, with the requisite accuracy, against all disorder or confusion. The irregularity is never, perhaps, so great as to destroy any species; but is often sufficient to involve the individuals in ruin and misery. (Hume [1] p. 210)

Even a finite deity ought to be able to do better than this. If the universe were the work of a designer we should not expect to find excess or defect in this part or that but everywhere 'the just temperament and medium' (Hume [1] p. 210).

The overall lesson which Hume is concerned to draw from these four considerations is that mere compatibility with the hypothesis of a supreme designer is not enough. What is wanted is positive evidence in favour of it. It is not that the considerations he adduces operate conclusively to destroy that hypothesis; but they do constitute stumbling-blocks, difficulties to be got over. It is not a sufficient answer to say that although there is evidence against a designer there is also evidence for one, and that we are therefore entitled to adopt a belief in such a designer. If our belief is to be based on evidence, and if there is evidence both for and against, we are not entitled to ignore one side of the evidence. What appears to be evidence of *dis*order, though it might be held to be on a careful interpretation not wholly incompatible with the hypothesis of a benevolent designer, could certainly never be regarded as helping to prove such a designer; yet it is among the evidence that needs to be taken into account.

It is important to stress that Hume's arguments on this point are aimed against the Argument from Design considered as an argument by analogy and an *a posteriori* argument – that is, an argument from empirical evidence. If we are to find grounds for belief in God in human experience, then we must be prepared to consider the whole of that experience and not just parts of it. Hume acknowledges that if we had prior knowledge of the goodness of God then it would be appropriate to look for a way round apparent evidence to the contrary. But if our knowledge of the goodness of God is supposed to be based upon the evidence, then we have no right merely to explain away evidence that tells against this hypothesis. What can justify us in doing this? The Argument is to be based only on the evidence, and there is nothing in the evidence itself to justify the adoption of selective methods of this kind.

Now it is certainly the case that proponents of the Argument have been at fault to the extent that they may have operated upon the evidence with undeclared (and perhaps by themselves only half-understood) principles of selection; and some of them may have been too ready to argue away unwelcome evidence of 'disorder' by allowing what they are trying to prove to determine the way in which such evidence is presented, namely, by seeing it as tending 'in the end' to serve some hidden purpose of good. But not all proponents of the Argument have been like this. Furthermore, from the religious point of view (as Paley saw, or at any rate sometimes saw), what is called the Argument from Design can be interpreted as dependent upon prior knowledge of God rather than as itself the basis of such knowledge. Hume's, and Mill's, views on the subject of the existence of evil in the universe bear upon the question of the existence of a benevolent designer rather than upon that of the existence of a designer.

Why should we put so much weight on the notion that the universe resembles the products of human contrivance? No doubt it does, in parts, but other parts of the universe, Hume suggests in the *Dialogues*, much more resemble animals and plants; and there may be yet other principles again which could be called upon to account for the universe – perhaps instinct rather than reason might be better.

If the analogy with animals and plants rather than that with machines is used to explain the universe, we cannot argue to a designer. Machines we know to be designed by rational agents. But that animals or plants have been designed by a rational agent, or by rational agents, is just what (in part) the Argument from Design is trying to prove; it cannot therefore be assumed. 'A tree bestows order and organisation on that tree which springs from it, without knowing the order: an animal, in the same manner, on its offspring: a bird, on its nest. . . . To say that all this order in animals and vegetables proceeds ultimately from design is begging the question' (Hume [1] p. 179). If the analogy with animals and plants could be shown to be a more plausible one than the analogy with machines, then the Argument from Design would be greatly weakened. Philo, in the *Dialogues*, does suppose it to be more plausible.

> The world plainly resembles more an animal or a vegetable, than it does a watch or a knitting-loom. Its cause, therefore, it is more probable, resembles the cause of the former. The cause of the former is generation or vegetation. The cause, therefore, of the world, we may infer to be some thing similar or analogous to generation or vegetation. (Hume [1] pp. 176–7)

Any suggestion that part, even a limited part, of the universe is better explained by means of some other analogy than that with a machine must operate against the Argument from Design in so far as that argument tends to assume that the analogy with machines applies throughout the universe (though, of course, we may not be able to detect it with equal ease in all parts of the universe). Philo is inserting the thin end of a wedge; and even if it were a thinner edge than he supposes, it could still damage the Argument.

Just how much weight we think it proper to put upon Hume's point depends on how impressive we find the suggested analogy with animals and plants. Hume is on strong ground to the extent that the analogy on which the Argument depends does undoubtedly come from a limited part of our experience – namely, our experience of the designing activity of human rational agents. Even if we consider ourselves the only inhabitants of Earth worth taking account of (and why should we?), are we right to consider only one aspect of our lives? We ourselves, like the animals, come into existence through 'generation'. Why should we suppose this to be something of little importance in the ultimate explanation of the universe?

Nevertheless, when one examines the way in which the analogy with animals and plants is presented in the *Dialogues*, the overall effect is not, I think, of an analogy that deserves to stand alongside the analogy with machines. Philo's development of it is in extravagant terms (a comet the seed of a world . . . a comet the egg of an animal – see Hume [1] p. 177), which assume that things happen in the universe that we in fact have no evidence for (it can only be the purest speculation that a comet 'sprouts up into a new system'). The Argument from Design attempts to explain what we *observe* in the universe. The explanation may involve speculation; but what is to be explained is hard empirical fact – the workings of the solar system or of the human eye – and not, as in Philo's examples, things that are not themselves hard empirical fact. We do not *observe* the sprouting up of new systems. Hume (through Philo) claims that we do not have evidence on which to establish 'any system of cosmogony' and that, this being so, all we can do is to base our view on the best analogy available. 'Is there any other rule than the greater similarity of the objects compared? And does not a plant or an animal, which springs from vegetation or generation, bear a stronger resemblance to the world, than does any artificial machine, which arises from reason and design?' (Hume [1] p. 177). The answer to the latter question would seem to be, simply, no. If our subject is the workings of heavenly bodies it is by no means evident that an analogy with plants or animals is better than an analogy with machines. Rather the contrary. The workings of the solar system are quite like the workings of a watch. The solar system does not strike the present writer, at any rate, as being more like a vegetable than a machine: it is not observed to grow, for one thing. If it is to be made a question, as Hume says it is, of which analogy is the more plausible, then Philo's opinion on this seems to me to be the wrong one. In either case, it is a matter of developing an analogy that is not going to be obvious to everyone – the solar system is certainly not *exactly* like a machine. It might be suggested that it is a matter of indifference which analogy (supposing that we are determined to have one at all) we adopt. Hume does not take this line; he requires that we adopt the most plausible analogy. Philo may be intending to ridicule the whole idea of applying to the universe any analogy based on our limited experience; but as our experience undoubtedly is experience of the universe, in some of its aspects, it is not clear that there is anything absurd at the outset in the general enterprise of trying to explain the universe in terms drawn from our experience. At the same time, it must be added, in fairness to Hume, that Philo mentions a significant circumstance in which experience is on his side. Reason is *observed* to arise from generation (Hume [1] p. 180), but never the reverse; generation might therefore more reasonably be said to explain rational activity than rational activity to explain generation – if we are to rely on experience.

Philo had previously drawn the analogy with animals (though not plants) in more moderate terms than those we have been considering. But it is not clear from what he there said either that this analogy is preferable to the analogy with machines.

A continual circulation of matter in [the universe] produces no disorder: A continual waste in every part is incessantly repaired: The closest sympathy is perceived throughout the entire system: And each part or member, in performing its proper offices, operates both to its own preservation and to that of the whole. The world, therefore, I infer, is an animal. . . . (Hume [1] pp. 170–1)

Only the second of these points looks as if it could not be made on the assumption that the universe is a machine: watches and the like are not self-repairing. The other points apply equally well on that assumption; with perhaps a change in terminology to something more neutral, as Philo has chosen to make them in words – 'sympathy', 'preservation' – which somewhat favour the animal analogy. Even the second point might, in fact, be interpreted in such a way as to be equally applicable under the machine analogy: it might be seen as referring to the loss of energy in a machine which is made up for by regular intake of fuel, etc.

It has sometimes been held – as by Descartes – that animals *are* machines. On that view there would be no difference between the two analogies under discussion. The subject called systems theory makes use of a general concept of system under which differences between the animate and the inanimate, or indeed between individuals and groups, are subordinate to the fact that they can all be studied as systems. From this point of view, again, an analogy with animals or plants might in important respects not be seen as significantly different from an analogy with machines.

But, of course, behind all the discussion in the *Dialogues* about whether the universe is more like an animal or plant than it is like a machine, there is an important general point: it is not only rational agents which bestow order. Given a machine, we know that the design it exhibits is the result of human rationality; but there are other kinds of design in our experience than the kind which we find in machines; and therefore there are other 'principles' of design. 'In this little corner of the world alone, there are four principles, *reason, instinct, generation, vegetation*, which are similar to each other, and are the causes of similar effects' (Hume [1] p. 178). Philo goes on, less plausibly, to say: 'Any one of these four principles above mentioned (and a hundred others which lie open to our conjecture) may afford us a theory, by which to judge of the origin of the world; and it is a palpable and egregious partiality, to confine our view entirely to that principle, by which our own minds operate' (Hume [1] p. 178). A hundred others? Out of this hundred, Hume chooses to apply the analogy of generation and vegetation to heavenly bodies and their workings. Philo's point might have seemed stronger if he had pressed the generation and vegetation analogy in respect of those aspects of the universe where it seems more appropriate: if he had pressed it, say, in the case of the workings of the eye or of the inner ear rather than in that of the workings of the solar system. But here the influence of Newton is to be seen. The version of the Argument from Design that Hume is assuming is a version which seeks the proof of

58

God in the heavenly bodies. It is presumably this that prevents Hume in this case from making the fullest use of his own objection to the Argument. Perhaps, however, Hume might reply by saying that he has answered this comment in advance: we have already noted his remark to the effect that we cannot suppose the workings of animals or plants to point to a designer without begging the question.

The Uniqueness of the Universe

Hume writes, in the *Enquiry*:

> It is only when two *species* of objects are found to be constantly conjoined, that we can infer the one from the other; and were an effect presented, which was entirely singular, and could not be comprehended under any known *species*, I do not see, that we could form any conjecture or inference at all concerning its cause. (Hume [2] p. 148)

The universe is 'entirely singular', or unique. We have not had experience of other universes with which we may compare this one. Indeed, the supposition that we might have had such experience is absurd. There is no class of universes. By definition, there can be only one universe, for the universe is everything that there is. How then, Hume is asking, can there be argument by analogy in this case? We only have argument by analogy in cases where we have a number of things which we see to resemble each other in certain respects and about which we can then argue, on the basis of these resemblances, that they probably resemble each other in another respect also. It is as if we should say: 'Universe B and Universe C and Universe D . . . had designers; Universe A (ours) resembles them in respects a and b and c . . .; it is likely that it resembles them also in the respect of having had a designer.' Such an argument simply could not work; for there is no such thing as a class of universes with the other members of which we may compare our own.

Hume is clearly right in saying that in some sense an argument by analogy involves *species* or classes of things. This, however, is not so fatal to the Argument from Design as he supposes. There are several possible lines of reply to Hume's objection.

(1) We may grant him that the Argument from Design argues from the universe considered as unique. But this does not mean that the Argument from Design cannot be an argument by analogy. True, there is no class of universes. But the class involved is not this non-existent class, anyway, but the class of machines. The one and only universe is seen to resemble a watch, or a knitting-loom, or, etc., in various respects; it is then concluded that it resembles them also in the respect that it had a designer.

(2) A second line of reply is provided if we now refuse to grant Hume his point that the Argument from Design argues from the universe considered as unique. The Argument can take a different form. It can be from particular parts of the universe considered separately – such as the Galaxy – in the case of each of which it is argued that it resembles, in certain respects, a machine. There is here no necessary assumption of the uniqueness of the universe, considered, as Hume put it, as 'an effect quite singular and unparalleled' requiring a cause 'no less singular and unparalleled' (Hume [2] p. 148). Admittedly, the Argument, if presented in this way, is liable to land us with a plurality of designers, but this is a separate objection, which we have discussed already.

(3) A third line of reply would be to question Hume's view that the uniqueness of the universe rules out the possibility of conjecture or inference about its cause. 'Universe' is ambiguous; so is 'unique'. There is a sense of 'universe' in which by definition the universe is unique. In this sense, 'universe' means 'everything that there is'. If this is a coherent notion at all (obscurity in the notion of 'thing', problems about countability, etc., make it possible that it is not an altogether coherent notion – though it is unnecessary to go into this matter here), then the universe no doubt must be unique; for there cannot be more than one collection of everything that there is. (It is worth remarking in parentheses that even this might be questioned. There can be more than one way of arranging the items in a collection, and therefore more than one way of arranging the items in a collection of 'everything that there is' and thus in this sense more than one collection of everything that there is.) There is, however, a second sense of 'universe' where it means, basically, the heavenly bodies, etc. – what is referred to, say, in the title of Sir James Jeans's book of popular

60

astronomy *The Mysterious Universe*. In this second sense, the universe is a collection of physical things – the planets, the stars, nebulae, etc. – and an account of it need not include reference to 'abstractions' like human wishes, virtues, etc., as would be necessary in an account of the universe taken in the first sense. (There is a sub-sense of this second sense, in which 'universe' can be regarded as a class-name: parts of the universe have themselves been called universes – compare the expression 'island universe'.) It is the second sense of 'universe' that seems to be intended in Hume's *Dialogues*. Now although it is no doubt true to say that the physical universe is the only one of its kind, it is not true to say that it is unique in any sense which would entail its being indescribable or which would preclude argument or speculation about its origins. 'Cosmologists', as Swinburne remarks, 'are reaching very well-tested scientific conclusions about the Universe as a whole, as are physical anthropologists about the origins of our human race, even though it is the only human race of which we have knowledge and perhaps the only human race there is' (Swinburne, p. 208).

God as an Entity

The notion of God as designer is clearly analogical, or meta-phorical. No one supposes that God is *literally* a designer; no one takes the notion of God as artist or artificer to mean that God is a kind of super-individual in an artist's smock or workman's overall. Even so, the Argument from Design fits most easily into a background of thought that inclines towards anthropo-morphism. It fits less easily into, for instance, a Tillichian view of God as 'the ground of our being'. Talk of God as designer, or artist, or artificer, is more readily intelligible if one supposes God an entity among entities, a Person in the sense of an identifiable individual (even though vastly superior to human persons). This is not the place to discuss rival views of God. It is clear, however, that if, as would be argued by most philo-sophers, it is a fundamental misunderstanding of the term 'God' to suppose it to refer to an entity among entities, the whole enterprise of drawing analogies between God and human designers is seen to be much less relevant to any questions con-cerning *God* than even Hume himself, let alone those he is criticising, supposed.

61

5 An Empirical Argument

As we have said earlier, the form of the Argument from Design that Hume was considering in the *Dialogues* owed much to Newton; Hume dealt with an argument which was supposed to be scientifically respectable: and part of what he, it seems, hoped to achieve was to show that this claim was unjustified. The question whether, or how far, the Argument from Design is scientifically respectable is also of importance in our own day, when the prestige of science is certainly not less than it has ever been; and although Hume's science is bound to seem unsophisticated from a present-day point of view, some at least of what he had to say on this question is still valuable. It should perhaps be said at once that the question whether or how far the Argument is scientifically respectable is a narrower question than that of whether or how far it is an empirical or *a posteriori* argument.

Is the Argument Scientifically Respectable?

Hume (in the *Enquiry*) used the expression 'the religious hypothesis'. If the Argument from Design is a scientific argument, we can expect it to issue in no more than the *hypothesis* of God the supreme designer. It would be untrue to the spirit of science to claim finality or certainty for its conclusions. The attitude of the religious believer, however, is not generally presented as that of one who entertains the hypothesis of God's existence, but rather as that of one who is convinced, has committed himself, or the like. However, it is a mistake to argue on the basis of this difference (though some do so argue) that no line of reasoning ending in the mere hypothesis of a supreme designer could have anything to do with the religious believer's faith in or commitment to God. The Argument from Design – if it were a scientific argument – could not provide a conclusion which is certainly true. But this would not prevent it from functioning as a preparation for faith or commitment. No doubt not many people have been argued into belief in the existence of God – and if they have, they ought not to have been. Nevertheless, reflection on the Argument from Design might at least induce a frame of mind congenial to faith.

Let us follow further the notion of 'the religious hypothesis'. There are difficulties for the view that this can be classed among scientific hypotheses. ('Science' is to be taken throughout as meaning 'natural science'. Neither Hume nor anyone else who considered this question was thinking in terms of the social or behavioural sciences.) If the religious hypothesis is a scientific hypothesis it must be possible to make predictions on the basis of it and it must be empirically falsifiable. What predictions can we make on the basis of the hypothesis that there is a supreme designer of the universe? An ordinary scientific hypothesis is used in the making of predictions of specific kinds. The religious hypothesis (it would seem) can only be the basis of a vague prediction that some design, or order, or benevolent purpose will be discovered if we examine this or that part of the universe that we have not yet examined. But precisely what design, what order, what purpose? That is something that the hypothesis, because of its highly general character, cannot tell us. The scientist would not be content with an hypothesis as general as this. He needs to be able to predict not that order or design will be found in this place or that; he needs to be able to predict what kind of order or design will be found there. If practically anything will fit the bill (and some design, some order, will surely be found by anyone who is looking for it), then the hypothesis is altogether too easy to confirm, too hard to falsify, for its own scientific good.

As we noted in the previous chapter, it is not clear what are the criteria for order and disorder, or for design and the absence of design, in the universe. One man's order may be another man's disorder. It is true that the design that the proponent of the Argument from Design claims to observe could be said, in a way, to be of a perfectly familiar kind: it is the design observable in the workings of the solar system or of the human eye, to take instances that have been widely used. But it is important to note that the Argument from Design puts a certain kind of interpretation upon such things. The scientist is not looking for *design*; his interest is in the ways in which things behave. To see design *in* the workings of the solar system or of the eye is to see more in their workings than the scientist would be likely to say he sees. That the workings of the solar system or of the eye are thus and thus (or are to be scientifically explained thus and thus) is a matter for empirical verification. That these workings exhibit design is something rather different – even where design is taken in the sense of design-A, let alone if it is taken in the sense of design-B. The scientist is not thinking in terms of a quite general notion of *design* but in terms of specific properties, principles and theories – unless, of course, he is for the moment philosophising or theologising about the universe, as some scientists sometimes do. The general notion of design is not one that the scientist needs to use; it is one, however, that the proponent of the Argument from Design can hardly do without. It would seem implausible to say that an argument is a scientific argument if an important component of it is a very general notion that a scientist need never use. The vagueness and generality of the notion of design – and, we may add, its unquantifiable character – disqualify the religious hypothesis as a scientific hypothesis.

We are, however, discussing the question how far the Argument from Design, or the religious hypothesis, are scientifically respectable; which can be interpreted as asking something rather less than whether the former actually is a scientific argument or the latter actually a scientific hypothesis. Is there some kind of parallel, some likeness, even if not a strong one, between the Argument from Design or the religious hypothesis on the one hand and scientific arguments or scientific hypotheses on the other? Hume, as we have noted, was inclined to say no. Swinburne, in the article we have already had occasion to refer to, has drawn some parallels between the Argument from Design and what may be regarded as proper or acceptable procedures in science. These parallels provide a possible basis for a defence, against Hume, of the view that the Argument from Design is not scientifically disreputable; though Swinburne himself does not argue in this way, and such a defence, as we shall see, cannot in fact be sustained.

(1) Swinburne points out that the conclusion of the Argument (to use Hume's phrase: 'the religious hypothesis'), namely, that there is a supreme designer of the universe, has 'an enormous simplifying effect on explanations of empirical matters' (p. 205). Instead of having to explain some things in mechanical terms,

65

others in terms of rational activity, everything would in the end be susceptible of an explanation of the same kind, namely as the work of a rational agent.

It is unquestionably an aim of science to reduce as far as possible the number of explanations necessary to explain any given set of phenomena, to bring ever more facts, hitherto supposed to need separate explanations, under a single explanatory umbrella. But simplicity, or fewness, of explanations is not enough. It would be a great gain in simplicity if all natural phenomena could be explained in terms of rational activity. To achieve this kind of simplicity, however, would not be a *scientific* gain. Swinburne says that 'normal scientific explanation would prove to be personal explanation' (p. 206) if the conclusion of the Argument from Design were true. Personal explanation is not scientific explanation. Although it is an aim of science – among others, with which, indeed, it can sometimes conflict – to achieve ever simpler explanation, this simplicity of explanation must be in recognisably scientific terms. Though science undoubtedly does seek ever simpler explanations, to be a simple explanation is not a sufficient condition of being a scientific explanation; there is non-scientific simplicity and, indeed, anti-scientific simplicity. It could only be an argument in favour of the scientific respectability of the Argument from Design that its conclusion, if accepted, would greatly simplify the explanation of many matters which scientists attempt to explain, if it could be shown that the kind of simplicity that was thus introduced was on other grounds recognisable as scientific. It is in fact, however, of a kind generally contrasted with scientific explanation.

(2) We have earlier referred to another point of Swinburne's: his mention of the practice of scientists of sometimes arguing to unobservables, as in the case of the argument to show that gases are made up of particles.

Science appeals to unobservables, but obviously not every appeal to unobservables is scientific; for instance, appeal to unobservables in explanation would include appeal to ghosts or spirits, but explanation in terms of ghosts or spirits is not scientific explanation. Swinburne himself indicates that not just any unobservable can be called upon in the construction of a scientific explanation. As he points out (in a passage quoted earlier – see above, p. 45), 'when observed As have a relation R

66

to observed Bs, it is often perfectly reasonable to postulate that observed A*s, *similar to* As have the same relation to unobserved and unobservable B*s *similar to* Bs' (p. 208; my italics). Now a divine rational agent is not *similar to* anything the natural sciences argue to.

(3) According to Hume (see Hume [1] pp. 160, 164), the order-producing rational agent invoked in explanation of the universe is itself in need of explanation. Swinburne points out (p. 208) that scientists also postulate entities (for example, molecules) that themselves may need to be accounted for but that nevertheless give simple and coherent explanations of many other things (and this is what justifies postulating them).

Molecules, however, seem to belong in scientific explanations as the activity of a divine rational agent does not. The activity of a divine rational agent is outside the range of things suitable to be postulated in scientific explanations. We may take Hume's point to be that if the Argument from Design gives an explanation of the universe that itself still calls for explanation, then this shows it to be an unscientific kind of explanation. Swinburne makes it plain that some scientific explanations also involve postulating things that themselves need explanation, which we may not be able to provide. My view on Hume's point, as has been indicated earlier in this book, is that explanation in terms of rational activity – which we can take for this purpose as including divine rational activity – is a kind of explanation that on the whole strikes us as *not* needing itself to be explained. But whether this be so or not, and whether science does or does not postulate entities in explanations that themselves are acknowledged to raise further, as yet unanswered, questions about explanation, does not bear upon the question whether the Argument from Design is a scientifically respectable argument. What really matters – to say it yet again – is not whether scientists use in explanations things that themselves need explanation, but rather *what kind* of thing they think it appropriate to use in explanations; and the notion of divine rational activity is not one that belongs among the notions that a natural scientist would think it appropriate to make use of. It is this that renders the Argument from Design unscientific.

I conclude that Hume, though his view of scientific explanation needs the corrections that Swinburne has provided in his article, was on the right lines in rejecting any implied claim to scientific respectability on behalf of the Argument from Design.

The Scientific and the Empirical

If the Argument is not a scientific argument, does this mean that it is not an empirical argument? Clearly not. There is no reason to suppose that all empirical arguments must pass the tests for scientific arguments. It is true that philosophical discussion of empirical argument does tend to put a fair amount of emphasis on discussion of the procedures of scientists; but this is because scientific arguments have a practical importance, a relatively systematic structure, and a history. The nature of scientific argument has long interested philosophers, and it is natural for them to look there for examples when the question of the nature of empirical reasoning is under consideration. It has seemed to some philosophers that scientific reasoning is the norm for empirical reasoning. But not every empirical argument is a scientific argument. Everyday inductive reasoning – for example, that in which, on the basis of a limited amount of observation, and probably a larger amount of hearsay, one concludes that red-haired women tend to be bad-tempered – is empirical but not scientific. Such a generalization could be scientifically based, of course, but for this there would need to be a carefully controlled investigation, involving comparison of the degree of bad-temperedness of women different in respect of hair colour but alike in other respects, such as their domestic situation. The arguments of historians are also empirical, but are distinguishable from scientific arguments by the fact that they are concerned with the explanation of single events rather than with that of classes of events. Some historians, it is true, have wanted to make historical investigation conform closely to scientific investigation.

In so far as it takes as its starting-point observation of things in nature, the Argument from Design is an empirical argument; and it is so irrespective of whether or not it is accounted also scientifically respectable.

It is no doubt possible to develop aspects of the Argument from Design in ways that would bring it closer to one of the other members of the standard trio of theistic 'proofs' – the Ontological Argument and the Cosmological Argument – and

68

thus also bring it closer to qualifying as an *a priori* rather than an empirical or *a posteriori* argument. Thus, if we take Descartes's version of the Ontological Argument (that the idea of God is the idea of God as all-perfect, and that if God is all-perfect he must possess the perfection of existence), we could develop an argument as follows: the idea of God is the idea of the All-Perfect; one of the perfections contained in this idea is that of perfect designer; but God could not design unless he existed; therefore God exists. This would be a bad argument to the existence of God, but I am not concerned here with its validity. The point is whether there would be any advantage in developing such an argument. Surely there would not. The virtue of the Argument from Design is precisely that it is different from the Ontological Argument and the Cosmological Argument. To try to remake it in a similar mould would be to destroy most of its point. It provides something that the other two standard 'proofs' do not provide: namely, a would-be *a posteriori* approach to the 'proof' of God. It fails; but at least it fails while being itself, not a copy of something else.

69

6 Conclusion

I have now completed my discussion of the three central themes that we noted at the outset: purpose, analogy, and the empirical character of the Argument. I shall in conclusion attempt a brief statement of what has emerged from the discussion of these themes, taking them in reverse order.

As an empirical argument, the Argument from Design, supposing it to be valid, could still not offer certainty. This is so whether or not we regard it as a scientific, or at least a scientifically respectable, argument. In fact it is not a scientific argument. The religious hypothesis fails to pass the test of being usable in the making of predictions that are empirically falsifiable; furthermore, the explanation that the Argument offers of design in the universe, an explanation in terms of a rational purposing mind, is of a kind foreign to natural science. Yet the question whether it is a scientific, or scientifically respectable, argument is still an important one to ask; for the Argument from Design is the only one of the standard trio of theistic proofs that is likely to make much appeal in a science-dominated age, and it is important to discover how far, if at all, the Argument can accommodate itself to the scientific attitude. Once, its scientific respectability might have seemed to be virtually secured by the single fact that it is an argument by analogy, for scientific argument seemed to Newton and his followers to be analogical argument (compare Hurlbutt, pp. 81, 145). This is no longer enough of a likeness. The connection between the Argument from Design and science is nevertheless a close one. It can be claimed (as it is by Swinburne) that the Argument is stronger if it is based not on particular adaptations (for example, the human eye) but on the kind of regularities that are summed up in general principles that hold good throughout the universe, namely, the laws of physical science.

If the Argument (assuming it for the moment to be not invalid on other grounds) cannot offer certainty in its conclusion, is it

71

therefore without value? Surely not. Its proponents, at their best, were reluctant to suppose that it could function as a demonstrative proof; though it must be admitted that this is something of a generalisation, as the writer whom I have specifically in mind is Paley, and it would perhaps be unwise to insist that his approach was widely shared. We have noted the cautiousness of Paley's approach. The Argument, as he sees it, has its place against a background of faith. It is most unlikely to prove God to someone who does not already believe in God. We can acknowledge, with Paley, that as a matter of fact those who read books (like Paley's own) or listen to sermons in which the Argument is expounded, will be people who are already believers in God. The Argument is not needed to convince them that God exists, for they are convinced of this already. The fact that it issues in a merely probable conclusion is from this point of view not a fatal shortcoming. It does not provide certainty, but its audience does not need it to provide certainty. The value of the Argument for them lies in its power to confirm belief, not create it, and in its power to set up a habit of mind, suitable for religious believers, in which there is a disposition to see design in the things about them. We may add the point that the Argument from Design, like the other theistic proofs, has the value of helping to make clear the idea of God. The point I am anxious to stress, though, is that the fact that the Argument cannot provide a conclusive demonstration of the existence of God is neither surprising nor a ground for condemning it. How could it provide certainty? In any case, the notion of 'evidence' of God at work in the universe is not to be separated from the religious believer's belief in God. What is seen as constituting evidence is dependent upon these beliefs; and the beliefs in turn, it seems, are supported by the evidence.

As an argument by analogy, the Argument from Design stands or falls by whether or not the analogy on which it relies is plausible. This is the analogy between aspects of the universe and machines, or between the universe as a whole and a vast machine. At any rate this is the analogy central to the Argument in the form in which Hume considered it, and Hume's treatment of it has established the pattern for philosophical discussion of the Argument ever since. Hume's objections are successful in ruling out a conclusion to the *infinite* God, and in showing that

72

we are hardly justified, on grounds of analogy alone, in concluding to a *benevolent* deity. But he does not, I think, succeed in his attempt to show that the analogy with machines is less plausible than an analogy with plants or animals (which, if it were established as against the analogy with machines, would make it impossible to argue to a divine designer without begging the question); and, further, he does not succeed in his claim that argument to a supreme designer is rendered impossible by the uniqueness of the universe. My reasons for these judgements on Hume are to be found in the chapter on analogy (Chapter 4). The amount of space given in this book to the discussion of Hume – either directly, in the shape of discussion of his *Dialogues*, or indirectly, in the shape of comments on the views of Swinburne, whose article on the Argument from Design itself takes the form of a critical discussion of Hume – I hope needs no justification. Hume's *Dialogues* constitute the classical source for criticism of the Argument from Design. What perhaps is more in need of justification is the omission of consideration of other writers – in particular, F. R. Tennant. I think it is true, however, that discussion of the Argument from Design in contemporary philosophical circles still centres around Hume's treatment of the Argument and hardly at all round Tennant's attempt to rehabilitate it. Professor A. Boyce Gibson writes of Tennant: 'In my considered view, the neglect of his great work, *Philosophical Theology* (1929), by philosophers interested in religion figures with the neglect of Whitehead by philosophers interested in science as one of the most unfortunate and gratuitous refusals of a heritage in the history of British thought' (Boyce Gibson, p. 152). In a book of the present kind, however, the proper thing, I believe, is to concentrate on those discussions of the Argument from Design that philosophers have chiefly been concerned with.

The explanation of the universe, or its parts, that the Argument from Design provides us with, is ultimately an explanation in terms of purpose. Here the most important question is undoubtedly whether there can be purpose without a purposing agent; that is, whether there can be design-B without a designer. Those who assert that there can be purpose without a purposing agent can be divided into (at least) two camps. On the one hand, there are those who would assert that 'purpose' in the universe is to be otherwise explained; that the explanation of natural events must always, and only, be given in causal or 'mechanistic' terms. Indeed, human behaviour itself (where 'behaviour' is used in a wide sense, to include what we call actions) can be fully accounted for in causal or mechanistic terms. On the other hand, there are those (like Professor Taylor) who want to retain teleological explanation, that is, explanation in terms of purposes or goals or ends, but who understand teleology as a feature of systems as a whole and as not suggesting any necessity to go outside those systems for an explanation of them. I have argued in Chapter 3 that it is essential to the Argument from Design that purpose in the sense of purposive action be kept independent of its products and of related notions such as that of means/end adaptation in nature. 'Mechanism', when it takes the form of denying any separate existence to purposing minds, offers in our day perhaps the most serious difficulty for the Argument from Design. The assessment of mechanism is a problem in the philosophy of mind, not in the philosophy of religion; this is indeed an illustration of the way in which work done in one branch of philosophy may be of relevance to the solution of problems in another. In particular, at the present time, when the philosophy of mind (following upon the work of Wittgenstein, Ryle and others) has come to occupy a central place in philosophy, it has become increasingly clear that work in that field has significance far outside its own immediate area. The future of the Argument from Design depends upon the refutation of mechanism. It is fortunately no part of my task to embark upon this, one of the most difficult problems of contemporary philosophy. (See Malcolm [1] and [2] for an attempted refutation of mechanism.) But it has, I hope, become clear from the discussion earlier in this book that the notion of a human purposing agent must be granted independent meaning and existence if the Argument from Design is to have any hope of being meaningful, let alone successful. The Argument from Design stands or falls by the analogy between human purposing agents, together with the products of their actions, and a presumed divine purposing agent (God), together with the products of *his* actions (the universe). There are difficulties along the way in the working out of the analogy, as we have seen; but the Argument from Design, as an argument by analogy, cannot even get off the ground unless it is possible to give sense to the notion of a *human* purposing mind. It is for this

74

reason that the challenge of mechanism constitutes a particular difficulty for the Argument from Design – a difficulty whose solution, as I have said, must be provided for, rather than by, the philosophy of religion.

Bibliography

St Thomas Aquinas, *Summa Theologica*, trans. Fathers of the English Dominican Province, vol. 1 (Burns Oates & Washbourne, London, n.d.).

A. Boyce Gibson, *Theism and Empiricism* (S.C.M. Press, London, 1970).

C. D. Broad, *Religion, Philosophy and Psychical Research* (Routledge & Kegan Paul, London, 1953).

Antony Flew: [1] *God and Philosophy* (Hutchinson, London, 1966).

[2] *Hume's Philosophy of Belief* (Routledge & Kegan Paul, London, 1961).

P. T. Geach, 'Aquinas', in G. E. M. Anscombe and P. T. Geach, *Three Philosophers* (Blackwell, Oxford, 1961).

David Hume: [1] *Dialogues concerning Natural Religion*, ed. N. Kemp Smith, 2nd ed. (Nelson, London, 1947).

[2] *Enquiries concerning the Human Understanding and concerning the Principles of Morals*, ed. L. A. Selby-Bigge, 2nd ed. (Clarendon Press, Oxford, 1966).

Robert H. Hurlbutt, *Hume, Newton, and the Design Argument* (Univ. of Nebraska Press, Lincoln, 1965).

Paul Janet, *Final Causes*, trans. W. Affleck, 2nd ed. (T. & T. Clark, Edinburgh, 1883).

Immanuel Kant, *Critique of Pure Reason*, trans. N. Kemp Smith (Macmillan, London, 1968).

Anthony Kenny, *The Five Ways* (Routledge & Kegan Paul, London, 1969).

Norman Malcolm: [1] 'Explaining Behaviour', in *Philosophical Review*, LXXVI (1967) 97–104.

[2] 'The Conceivability of Mechanism', in *Philosophical Review*, LXXVII (1968) 45–72.

J. S. Mill, *Three Essays on Religion* (Longmans, Green, London, 1875).

William Paley, *Natural Theology*, in vol. III of *The Complete Works of William Paley, D.D.* (G. Cowie, London, 1825).

J. J. C. Smart, 'The Existence of God', in Antony Flew and
Alasdair MacIntyre (eds), *New Essays in Philosophical Theology*
(S.C.M. Press, London, 1955).

R. G. Swinburne, 'The Argument from Design', in *Philosophy*,
XLIII (1968) 199–212.

Charles Taylor, *The Explanation of Behaviour* (Routledge &
Kegan Paul, London, 1964).

F. R. Tennant, *Philosophical Theology*, 2 vols (Cambridge U.P.,
1928–30).

Brian Wicker, *God and Modern Philosophy* (Darton, Longman &
Todd, London, 1964).